Cooking for Christmas

STEP-BY-STEP

Cooking for Christmas

Sue Maggs

Photographs by Karl Adamson

LORENZ BOOKS

LONDON • NEW YORK • SYDNEY • BATH

First published in 1995 by Lorenz Books

© Anness Publishing Limited 1995

Lorenz Books is an imprint of
Anness Publishing Limited
1 Boundary Row
London SE1 8HP

ISBN 1 85967 145 4

Distributed in Australia by Reed Editions

A CIP catalogue record is available from the British Library.

Publisher: Joanna Lorenz
Series Editor: Lindsay Porter
Designer: Lilian Lindblom
Photographer: Karl Adamson

Measurements
Three sets of measurements have been provided, in the following order:
metric, imperial and US cups. It is essential that one set of
measurements is followed throughout each recipe. Where conversions
result in an awkward number, these have been rounded for convenience,
but will still provide a successful result.

Printed and bound in Hong Kong

CONTENTS

INTRODUCTION

Christmas is a time for celebrations, a time for entertaining family and friends and sharing the best of festive food and 'goodies' with them. Cooking for Christmas can seem like entering a marathon, though, and not even the keenest cook wants to spend the festive season imprisoned in the kitchen: the whole family should be together as much as possible. This book includes recipes, cook-ahead instructions and freezer-tips to make the festive period as easy and as enjoyable as possible. As this is the season for entertaining, all the recipes will serve eight people; of course, the recipes can be halved or doubled-up, if necessary.

To make life easier for yourself over the busy Christmas period, try to prepare as much as possible in advance and finish off or reheat on the day. Planning is essential: use the suggested menus provided or make up your own menus. Use your menus to draw up shopping lists, and allow yourself plenty of time to shop. Don't forget to allow time to pick up last-minute fresh foods and try to prepare and cook as much in advance as possible. Make use of your freezer, if you have one. Desserts, pastries, and stuffings can all be made ahead and frozen.

Recipes for non-meat eaters have also been included, because so many families have one or more vegetarians to cater for at Christmas. Most of these are also very good served with any of the meat dishes as an accompaniment, and even confirmed meat-lovers might appreciate the variety of textures, colours and flavours provided by these interesting vegetable recipes, as a change.

On the big day, allow yourself plenty of time and don't be afraid to draft in the rest of the family to help. All this should give you the freedom to enjoy the company of family and friends.

Useful Techniques

This section contains mini-recipes and lots of tips and useful information on cooking techniques to help you sail through the holiday season. It's worth sitting down a few weeks in advance to make a few plans about what you are going to cook and when is the best time to start.

This section is arranged according to such a plan: it begins with home-made preserves to fill festive jars that will remind you of the treats to come as you make your preparations – you could even give them as presents. Then there are icings you make yourself to decorate a home-made or bought cake. Don't forget the pudding. The recipe on page 72–73 can be made up to a month in advance.

Once the festive season gets under way, there are plenty of opportunities for parties and get-togethers of all sorts. The recipes in the Cold Buffets chapter are designed for trouble-free entertaining for large numbers. In this section you will find ideas for

cocktail snacks that will supplement the buffet or be perfect for when the neighbours drop round. Ideas for Christmas drinks are also given, including low- and no-alcohol ideas.

On Christmas Day itself, the information on turkey and its accompaniments will give you all you need for a triumphant celebratory dinner. Follow the turkey with your pudding, accompanied by one of the delicious sweet sauces.

Lastly in this section are some suggested menus for all kinds of occasions over the holiday season. Use them to take the hassle out of planning, or as a starting point for your own ideas.

Spiced Cranberry and Orange Relish

This is excellent with roast turkey, goose or duck.

Makes about 450 g/1 lb

INGREDIENTS
225 g/8 oz/1½ cups fresh cranberries
1 onion, finely chopped
150 ml/¼ pint/⅔ cup port
115 g/4 oz/½ cup caster sugar
finely grated rind and juice of 1 orange
2.5 ml/½ tsp English mustard powder
¼ tsp ground ginger
¼ tsp ground cinnamon
5 ml/1 tsp cornflour
50 g/2 oz/⅓ cup raisins

2 Mix the orange juice, mustard powder, spices and cornflour together. Stir them into the cranberries.

1 Put the cranberries, onion, port and sugar in a pan. Cook gently for 10 minutes, until tender.

3 Add the raisins and orange rind. Allow to thicken over the heat, stirring with a wooden spoon and then simmer for 2 minutes. Cool, cover and chill ready for serving.

Curried Fruit Chutney

Make this well ahead of Christmas, to serve with cold sliced turkey and ham.

Makes about 1.2 kg/2½ lb

INGREDIENTS
225 g/8 oz dried apricots
225 g/8 oz dried peaches
225 g/8 oz dates, stoned
225 g/8 oz/1⅓ cups raisins
1–2 garlic cloves, crushed
225 g/8 oz/1 generous cup soft light
  brown sugar
300 ml/½ pint/1¼ cups white malt
  vinegar
300 ml/½ pint/1¼ cups water
5 ml/1 tsp salt
10 ml/2 tsp mild curry powder

1 Put all the ingredients in a large pan, cover and simmer very gently for 10–15 minutes, or until tender.

2 Chop or mince the mixture coarsely in batches in a food processor.

3 Spoon into clean jam jars. Seal the jars and label them. Store in a cool place for 4 weeks before using.

Ginger, Date, and Apple Chutney

Make this well ahead and store it in airtight jars. Serve with cold sliced meats or pies.

Makes about 1.5 kg/3½ lb

INGREDIENTS
450 g/1 lb cooking apples
450 g/1 lb dates
225 g/8 oz dried apricots
115 g/4 oz glacé ginger, chopped
1–2 garlic cloves, crushed
225 g/8 oz/1⅓ cups sultanas
225 g/8 oz/1 generous cup soft light
  brown sugar
5 ml/1 tsp salt
300 ml/½ pint/1¼ cups white malt
  vinegar

2 Put all the fruit together in a large pan, with the remaining ingredients. Cover and simmer gently for 10–15 minutes, or until tender.

1 Peel, core and chop the apples. Stone the dates and chop them roughly. Chop the apricots.

3 Spoon into clean jam jars. Seal the jars and label them. Store in a cool place for 4 weeks before using.

Lining a Cake Tin

Rich, fruity Christmas cakes must be baked in a lined tin. The technique is very straightforward.

1 Place the cake tin on a double piece of greaseproof paper, draw around the base of the tin and cut out two circles to fit inside the tin.

2 Measure the circumference of the tin with a piece of string and cut a double strip of greaseproof paper slightly longer than the circumference. Fold over 2.5 cm/1 in along one long side. Cut diagonal slits in the folded-over part, up to the fold line.

3 Grease the tin. Place one circle of paper in the base of the tin. Fit the double-strip around the tin, neatly arranging the snipped edge over the bottom of the tin so it fits flat. Place the second circle of greaseproof paper on top, to make a smooth base.

Fondant Icing

This icing can be used for modelling decorations as well as covering a cake.

Makes enough to cover a 20 cm/8 in round cake

INGREDIENTS
60 ml/4 tbsp water
15 g/½ oz/1 tbsp powdered gelatine
10 ml/2 tsp liquid glucose
500 g/1¼ lb/5 cups icing sugar

1 Put the water in a small bowl and sprinkle over the gelatine. Leave to soak for 2 minutes. Place the bowl in a pan of hot water and leave to dissolve over a very gentle heat.

2 Remove the bowl from the hot water and add the liquid glucose to the dissolved gelatine.

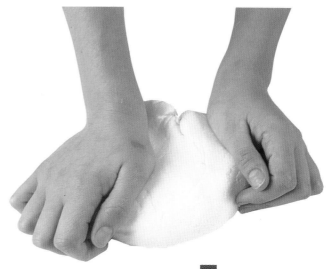

3 Sift the icing sugar into a bowl and add the gelatine mixture. Mix thoroughly and then knead to a smooth paste. Wrap in clear film until ready to use.

Almond Paste

Use almond paste as a base for royal or fondant icing. It will help to keep the cake moist.

Makes enough to cover a 20 cm/8 in round cake

INGREDIENTS
350 g/12 oz/4 cups ground almonds
175 g/6 oz/⅞ cup caster sugar
175 g/6 oz/1½ cups icing sugar
5 ml/1 tsp lemon juice
¼ tsp almond essence
1 egg

2 With a fork, beat the lemon juice, almond essence and egg together in a small bowl. Stir them into the dry ingredients.

1 Sift the ground almonds, caster sugar and icing sugar together into a bowl.

3 Knead together until smooth and wrap in clear film until needed.

Royal Icing

This icing will dry very hard and is a wonderful covering for cakes.

Makes enough to cover a 20 cm/8 in round cake

INGREDIENTS
2 egg whites
5 ml/1 tsp lemon juice
5 ml/1 tsp glycerine (optional)
450 g/1 lb icing sugar

2 Gradually sift in enough icing sugar to make a thick paste.

1 In a large bowl, beat the egg whites, lemon juice and glycerine (if using) together with a fork.

3 Using a wooden spoon, beat in the remaining icing sugar until the icing forms stiff peaks. Cover with clear film until ready to use.

Nutty Cheese Balls

These tasty morsels are perfect for nibbling with drinks.

Makes 32

INGREDIENTS
115 g/4 oz cream cheese
115 g/4 oz Roquefort cheese
115 g/4 oz/1 cup chopped walnuts
chopped fresh parsley, to coat
paprika, to coat
salt and freshly ground black pepper

1 Beat the two cheeses together until smooth using an electric beater.

2 Stir in the chopped walnuts and season with salt and pepper.

3 Shape into small balls (about a rounded teaspoonful each). Chill on a baking sheet until firm.

4 Roll half the balls in the chopped parsley and half in the paprika. Serve on cocktail sticks.

Salami and Olive Cheese Wedges

Use good quality salami for best results.

Makes 24

INGREDIENTS
225 g/8 oz cream cheese
5 ml/1 tsp paprika
2.5 ml/½ tsp English mustard powder
50 g/2 oz/2 tbsp stuffed green olives, chopped
225 g/8 oz sliced salami
sliced olives, to garnish

2 Spread the salami slices with the olive mixture and stack five slices on top of each other. Wrap in clear film and chill until firm. With a sharp knife, cut each stack into four wedges. Garnish with additional sliced olives and serve with a cocktail stick through each wedge, to hold the slices together.

1 Beat the cream cheese with the paprika and mustard and mix well. Stir in the chopped olives.

Spiced Mixed Nuts

Spices are a delicious addition to mixed roasted nuts.

Makes 350 g/12 oz/2 cups

INGREDIENTS
115 g/4 oz/⅔ cup brazil nuts
115 g/4 oz/⅔ cup cashew nuts
115 g/4 oz/⅔ cup almonds
2.5 ml/½ tsp mild chilli powder
2.5 ml/½ tsp ground coriander
2.5 ml/½ tsp salt
25 g/1 oz/2 tbsp butter, melted

1 Preheat the oven to 180°C/350°F/ Gas 4. Put all the nuts and spices and the salt on to a baking tray and mix well.

2 Pour over the melted butter and bake for 10–15 minutes, stirring until golden brown.

3 Drain on kitchen paper and allow to cool before serving.

Herby Cheese Biscuits

Use a selection of festive shapes for cutting out these biscuits.

Makes 32

INGREDIENTS
350 g/12 oz/3 cups plain flour
2.5 ml/½ tsp cayenne pepper
5 ml/1 tsp English mustard powder
175 g/6 oz/¾ cup butter
175 g/6 oz strong Cheddar cheese, grated finely
15 ml/1 tbsp mixed dried herbs
1 egg, beaten
salt and freshly ground black pepper

1 Preheat the oven to 200°C/400°F/ Gas 6. Sift the flour, cayenne pepper and mustard powder together into a bowl or food processor.

2 Rub the butter into the flour and add the cheese, herbs and seasoning. Stir in the beaten egg to bind, and knead to a smooth dough.

3 On a lightly floured work surface, roll the dough out thinly. Stamp it into small biscuits with cutters. Bake for 10–15 minutes, or until golden. Cool on a wire rack. Store in an airtight container.

Mulled Red Wine

Excellent to serve on a cold winter's evening; it will really get the party started.

Makes 900 ml/1½ pints/2½ cups

INGREDIENTS
1 bottle red wine
75 g/3 oz/6 tbsp soft light brown sugar
2 cinnamon sticks
1 lemon, sliced
4 whole cloves
150 ml/¼ pint/⅔ cup brandy or port
lemon slices, to serve

I Put all the ingredients, except the brandy or port, into a large pan. Bring the wine to the boil to dissolve the sugar. Remove, cover the pan and leave it to stand for 5 minutes, to allow the flavours to infuse.

2 Strain to remove the spices and lemon slices.

3 Add the brandy and serve warm, with a fresh slice of lemon.

Sparkling Cider Cup

This is a very refreshing, sparkling drink, best served as cold as possible.

Makes 2.6 litres/4½ pints/10½ cups

INGREDIENTS
1 orange
1 lemon
1 apple
1 litre/1¾ pints/4 cups sparkling
   cider, chilled
1 litre/1¾ pints/4 cups lemonade,
   chilled
600 ml/1 pint/2½ cups apple juice,
   chilled
fresh mint sprigs, to serve

2 Add the cider, lemonade and apple juice. Serve cold with sprigs of fresh mint.

I Slice all the fruit into a large bowl.

Spiced Fruit Cocktail

This non-alcoholic fruit drink is a real treat.

Makes 2 litres/3¹/₂ pints/8³/₄ cups

INGREDIENTS
600 ml/1 pint/2½ cups orange juice,
    chilled
300 ml/½ pint/1¼ cups pineapple
    juice, chilled
pared rind and juice of 1 lemon
4 whole cloves
1 cinnamon stick, broken into pieces
50 g/2 oz/4 tbsp caster sugar
orange slices
ice cubes
600 ml/1 pint/2½ cups sparkling
    mineral water, chilled
600 ml/1 pint/2½ cups ginger ale,
    chilled

1 Mix the orange and pineapple juices together in a large bowl. Add the lemon rind and juice, spices and sugar. Chill.

2 Put the orange slices and ice cubes in a serving bowl. Strain the fruit juice mixture into the bowl. Add the mineral water and ginger ale.

Fruit Punch

This is a quick punch to assemble. Make sure that all the ingredients are well chilled.

Makes 2.5 litres/4¹/₄ pints/10¹/₄ cups

INGREDIENTS
1 bottle white wine, chilled
1 bottle red wine, chilled
45 ml/3 tbsp orange-flavoured liqueur
1 orange, cut in quarters and sliced
seedless grapes
ice cubes
1 litre/1³/₄ pints/4 cups lemonade

2 Add the orange pieces, grapes and ice, and finally the lemonade.

1 Empty the wines and liqueur into a large bowl.

Prune, Orange and Nut Stuffing

You could also finely chop the reserved turkey liver and mix it into this stuffing.

Serves 8 (enough to stuff a 4.5 kg/10 lb turkey)

INGREDIENTS
115 g/4 oz/1 cup stoned prunes
60 ml/4 tbsp red wine or sherry
1 onion, finely chopped
25 g/1 oz/2 tbsp butter
225 g/8 oz/5 cups fresh white
    breadcrumbs
finely grated rind of 1 orange
2 eggs, beaten
30 ml/2 tbsp chopped fresh parsley
15 ml/1 tbsp mixed dried herbs
large pinch of ground allspice
large pinch of grated nutmeg
115 g/4 oz/1 cup chopped walnuts
    or pecans
2 celery sticks, finely chopped
salt and freshly ground black pepper

1 Put the prunes and red wine or sherry in a small pan, cover and simmer gently until tender. Set aside to cool.

2 Cook the onion gently in the butter until tender, about 10 minutes.

3 Cut each prune into four pieces. Mix all the ingredients in a large bowl and season well with salt and pepper.

Rice, Mushroom and Leek Stuffing

The rice gives this stuffing a crumbly, light texture.

Serves 8 (enough to stuff a 4.5 kg/10 lb turkey)

INGREDIENTS
115 g/4 oz/½ cup rice
25 g/1 oz/2 tbsp butter
225 g/8 oz leeks, washed and sliced
225 g/8 oz mushrooms, chopped
2 celery sticks, finely chopped
50 g/2 oz/½ cup chopped walnuts
1 egg, beaten
60 ml/4 tbsp chopped fresh parsley
10 ml/2 tsp dried thyme
finely grated rind of 1 lemon
225 g/8 oz apple, peeled, cored
    and diced
salt and freshly ground black pepper

2 Mix all the remaining ingredients thoroughly together in a large bowl and season with salt and pepper.

1 Cook the rice in plenty of boiling, salted water for 12 minutes until tender. Drain the rice thoroughly and let it cool. Melt the butter in a frying-pan and cook the leeks and mushrooms until tender. Increase the heat and cook to evaporate any remaining moisture in the pan. Set aside to cool.

3 Add the rice, and the leek and mushroom mixture to the bowl and mix together thoroughly.

Making Bacon Rolls

If you want to wrap stoned prunes or chicken livers inside each rasher cut the bacon rashers in half after stretching them.

 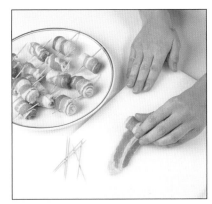

1 Remove the rind from the rashers of bacon and stretch them with the back of a large knife.

2 Roll the rashers up neatly.

3 Skewer the bacon rolls with cocktail sticks. Grill the rolls until crisp, turning them half-way through cooking.

Roasting Potatoes

Floury potatoes make the best crisp roast potatoes. Garlic or rosemary can be added to the oil, to flavour the potatoes during cooking.

1 Preheat the oven to 200°C/400°F/ Gas 6. Peel the potatoes and cut large potatoes in half. Parboil them for 10 minutes. Drain. Score the surface of each potato with a fork. Roll them in flour and tap them to remove any excess. Heat 2.5 cm/1 in olive oil in a shallow roasting tin until smoking hot.

2 Put the potatoes in the hot oil and baste them to coat them in oil. Roast for about an hour.

3 Baste and turn the potatoes twice during cooking. Drain them on kitchen paper and sprinkle them with salt.

Carving a Turkey

1 First remove the leg, by cutting the skin between the breast and leg. Press the leg flat, to expose the joint. Cut between the bones through the joint.

2 Cut the leg in two, through the joint.

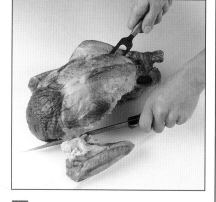

3 Carve the leg into slices.

4 Remove the wing, cutting through the joint in the same way as for the leg.

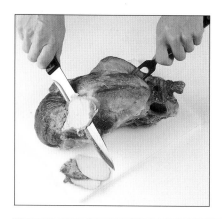

5 Carve the breast in thin slices, starting at the front of the breast. Then carve slices from the back of the breast, alternating the slices between front and back, until all the breast has been carved.

Times for Roasting Turkey

When choosing a turkey for Christmas, you should allow about 450 g/1 lb of dressed (plucked and oven-ready) bird per head. A good sized turkey to buy for Christmas is 4.5 kg/10 lb. This will serve about 12 people, with leftovers for the following day.

Thaw a frozen turkey, still in its bag, on a plate at room temperature (18–21°C/65–70°F) until the legs are flexible and there are no ice crystals in the cavity of the bird. Remove the giblets from the cavity as soon as the bird has thawed enough.

Oven-ready weight	Thawing time	Number of servings	Cooking time
3.5 kg/8 lb	18 hours	8–10 people	2½–3½ hours
4.5 kg/10 lb	19 hours	12–14 people	3½–4 hours
5.5 kg/12 lb	20 hours	16–18 people	3¾–4½ hours
6.3 kg/14 lb	24 hours	18–20 people	4–5 hours

These times apply to a turkey weighed after stuffing and at room temperature. Cook in a moderate oven, 180°C/350°F/Gas 4, covered with butter and bacon rashers and loosely covered with foil.

To test whether the turkey is fully cooked, push a skewer into the thickest part of the leg and press the flesh; the juices should run clear and free from any blood. The legs take longer than the breast to cook; keep the breast covered with foil until the legs are cooked. The foil can be removed for the final hour of cooking, to brown and crisp the skin. The turkey should be basted with the juices from the roasting tin, every hour of cooking.

Plan for the turkey to be ready 15–20 minutes before you want to serve dinner. Remove it from the oven and allow the flesh to relax before carving it.

Brandy or Rum Butter

Serve with Christmas pudding or mince pies.

Makes about 175 g/6 oz/³/₄ cup

INGREDIENTS
75 g/3 oz/6 tbsp unsalted butter
75 g/3 oz/6 tbsp caster sugar
finely grated rind of 1 small orange
45 ml/3 tbsp brandy or rum

1 Whisk the butter, sugar and orange rind together until soft and fluffy.

2 Gradually whisk in the brandy or rum. Chill until ready to serve.

Whisky Sauce

This is another delicious accompaniment to Christmas pudding or mince pies.

Makes about 600 ml/1 pint/2¹/₂ cups

INGREDIENTS
30 ml/2 tbsp cornflour
600 ml/1 pint/2½ cups milk
25 g/1 oz/2 tbsp caster sugar
60 ml/4 tbsp whisky
grated nutmeg

1 In a small bowl, mix the cornflour with 15 ml/1 tbsp of the milk to make a smooth paste.

2 Bring the remaining milk to the boil, remove from the heat and pour a little on to the cornflour mixture and mix the cornflour into the pan.

3 Return to the heat, stirring constantly until thickened. Simmer for 2 minutes. Turn off the heat and add the sugar and whisky. Pour into a serving jug and sprinkle with the grated nutmeg.

SUGGESTED MENUS

Christmas Dinner for 8 People

Cheese and Pesto Pasties

Roast Turkey, stuffing balls, chipolata sausages, Bacon Rolls and gravy

Roast Potatoes and Brussels Sprouts with Chestnuts and Carrots

Steamed Christmas Pudding with Whisky Sauce

Vegetarian Christmas Dinner for 8 People

Christmas Salad with bought mini bread rolls

Cheese and Spinach Flan or Vegetarian Christmas Pie

Vegetable Crumble or Brussels Sprouts with Chestnuts and Carrots

Crunchy Apple and Almond Flan

New Year's Eve Party for 8 People

Smoked Salmon Salad

Roast Goose with Caramelized Apples and Port ana Orange Gravy

Gratin Dauphinois and Sweet and Sour Red Cabbage

Chocolate and Chestnut Yule Log

Hot Fork-supper for 12 People

Roquefort Tartlets and Potted Stilton with Herbs and Melba toast

Spiced Lamb with Fruit Pilaf

Sweet and Sour Red Cabbage

Iced Praline Torte and Ruby Fruit Salad

Boxing Day Lunch for 12 People

Warm Prawn Salad with bought herb and garlic bread

Baked Gammon with Cumberland Sauce

Vegetable Gnocchi

De Luxe Mincemeat Tart

Cold Buffet Lunch for 12 People

Layered Salmon Terrine

Fillet of Beef with Ratatouille

Turkey Rice Salad

Ginger Trifle and Almond Mincemeat Tartlets

Coundown to Christmas

This at-a-glance time-table will help you plan and organize your Christmas cooking. If you have chosen your menu from one of those suggested previously, the table below suggests when the components may be prepared.

Late Autumn
Make preserves and relishes such as Cranberry and Orange Relish or Curried Fruit Chutney to serve with cold meats.

November
Second week
Make Moist and Rich Christmas Cake.

Third week
Feed Moist and Rich Christmas Cake (optional).

Fourth week
Make Christmas Pudding.
Decide on Christmas dinner menu.
Order turkey, goose, beef or ham.
Continue to feed Moist and Rich Christmas Cake (optional).

December
First week
Make Light Jewelled Fruit Cake.
Make mincemeat for De Luxe Mincemeat Tart.
Continue to feed Moist and Rich Christmas Cake (optional).
Compile complete shopping list for main Christmas meals under headings for different stores, or for the various counters at the supermarket.
Continue to add to list throughout the week.

Second week
Make Almond Paste to cover Moist and Rich Christmas Cake.
Shop for dry goods such as rice, dried fruits and flour.
Order special bread requirements.
Order milk, cream and other dairy produce.
Make Brandy Butter.

Third week
Make Cheese and Pesto Pasties and other pastry-type cocktail savouries and freeze.
Cover Moist and Rich Christmas Cake with royal icing, leave one day, then cover and store.

Fourth week
Shop for chilled ingredients.
Buy wines and other drinks.

21 December
Check thawing time for frozen turkey, duck, beef or other meat.
Large turkeys (11.5 kg/25 lb) need 86 hours (3½ days) to thaw in the refrigerator, or 40 hours at room temperature.
Make a note to take the meat from the freezer at the appropriate time.

23 December
Shop for fresh vegetables, if not possible to do so on 24 December.
Make Cheese and Spinach Flan and freeze, if not making on Christmas Day.
Make Crunchy Apple and Almond Flan.

24 December
Shop for fresh vegetables, if possible.
Assemble Christmas Salad and refrigerate dressing separately.
Make stuffing for poultry.
Cook poultry giblets to make gravy.
Defrost Cheese and Pesto Pasties.
Prepare Bacon Rolls by threading them on to cocktail sticks.
Make Whisky Sauce to serve with Christmas Pudding.

Christmas Day
This timetable is planned for Christmas Dinner to be served at 2.00pm. If you wish to serve it at a different time, please adjust the times accordingly.

Stuff poultry. Make forcemeat balls with any left-over stuffing, or spoon it into greased ovenproof dishes.
Set table, if not already done.

Put steamer or large saucepan on cooker and bring water to the boil.
Put Christmas Pudding on to steam.

To cook a 4.5 kg/10 lb turkey
9.05am	Set oven to 220°C/ 425°F/Gas 7.
9.25am	Put turkey in oven.
9.45am	Reduce heat to 180°C/ 350°F/Gas 4.

	Baste turkey now and at frequent intervals.
12.15pm	Put potatoes around meat. Remove foil from turkey and baste again. Turn the potatoes.
12.45pm	Increase heat to 200°C/ 400°F/Gas 6. Put any dishes of stuffing in oven.
1.45pm	Remove turkey and potatoes from oven, put on heated dish, cover with foil and keep warm. Make gravy and grill bacon rolls.

To cook vegetarian menu
11.15am	Make pastry for Cheese and Spinach Flan, if not cooking from frozen. (If you are making Christmas Pie, begin 20 minutes earlier to allow time to chill the assembled pie.)
11.45am	Put pastry in the fridge and chill. Prepare sprouts for Brussels Sprouts with Chestnuts and Carrots.
12.15pm	Preheat oven for Cheese and Spinach Flan. Remove pastry from fridge and assemble. (For Christmas Pie, chill assembled dish for 20 minutes before baking. Preheat oven 10 minutes before removing pie from fridge.)
1.00pm	Put flan or pie in oven.
1.20pm	Simmer chestnuts for 10 minutes.
1.30pm	Simmer sprouts for 5 minutes.
1.35pm	Simmer carrots for 5 minutes.
1.40pm	Gently reheat all vegetables together.
1.45pm	Remove flan or pie from oven.
2.00pm	Serve first course.

Cheese and Pesto Pasties

These pasties can be made ahead and frozen uncooked. Freeze them in a single layer and then transfer them to a freezer-proof container. To serve, arrange the pasties on baking trays, brush them with oil and bake from frozen for 5–10 minutes longer than the recommended time.

Serves 8

INGREDIENTS
225 g/8 oz frozen chopped spinach
30 ml/2 tbsp pine nuts
60 ml/4 tbsp pesto sauce
115 g/4 oz Gruyère cheese
50 g/2 oz/½ cup grated Parmesan cheese
2 × 275 g/10 oz packet of frozen filo pastry, thawed
30 ml/2 tbsp olive oil
salt and freshly ground black pepper

Parmesan

olive oil

spinach

pesto sauce

filo pastry

pine nuts

1 Preheat the oven to 190°C/375°F/Gas 5. Prepare the filling; put the frozen spinach into a pan, and heat gently to defrost, breaking it up as it defrosts. Increase the heat to drive off any excess moisture. Transfer to a bowl and cool.

2 Put the pine nuts into a frying-pan and stir over a very low heat until they are lightly toasted. Chop them and add them to the spinach, with the pesto and Gruyère and Parmesan cheeses. Season to taste.

3 Unwrap the filo pastry and cover it with clear film and a damp tea towel (to prevent it from drying out). Take one sheet at a time and cut it into 5 cm/2 in wide strips. Brush each strip with oil.

4 Put a teaspoon of filling on one end of each strip of pastry. Fold the end over in a triangle, enclosing the filling.

5 Continue to fold the triangle over and over again until the end of the strip is reached. Repeat with the other strips, until all the filling has been used up.

6 Place the pasties on baking trays, brush them with oil and bake for 20–25 minutes, or until golden brown. Cool on a wire rack. Serve warm.

Christmas Salad

A light first course that can be prepared ahead and assembled just before serving.

Serves 8

INGREDIENTS
mixed red and green lettuce leaves
2 sweet pink grapefruit
1 large or 2 small avocados, peeled
    and cubed

FOR THE DRESSING
90 ml/6 tbsp light olive oil
30 ml/2 tbsp red wine vinegar
1 garlic clove, crushed
5 ml/1 tsp Dijon mustard
salt and freshly ground black pepper

FOR THE CARAMELIZED ORANGE PEEL
4 oranges
50 g/2 oz/4 tbsp caster sugar
60 ml/4 tbsp cold water

lettuce leaves

red wine vinegar

oranges

avocados

grapefruit

olive oil

1 To make the caramelized peel, using a vegetable peeler, remove the rind from the oranges in thin strips and reserve the fruit. Scrape away the white pith from the underside of the rind with a sharp knife, and cut the rind in fine shreds.

2 Put the sugar and water in a small pan and heat gently until the sugar has dissolved. Then add the shreds of orange rind, increase the heat and boil steadily for 5 minutes, until the rind is tender. Using two forks, remove the orange rind from the syrup and spread it out on a wire rack to dry. (This can be done the day before.) Reserve the syrup to add to the dressing.

3 Wash and dry the lettuce and tear the leaves into bite-sized pieces. Wrap them in a clean, damp tea towel and keep them in the fridge. Cut the pith off the oranges and grapefruit. Holding the fruit over a bowl to catch any juice, cut them into segments, removing all the pith.

4 Put all the dressing ingredients into a screw-top jar and shake the jar vigorously to emulsify the dressing. Add the reserved orange-flavoured syrup and adjust the seasoning to taste. Arrange the salad ingredients on individual plates with the avocados, spoon over the dressing and scatter on the caramelized peel.

Warm Prawn Salad with Spicy Marinade

The ingredients can be prepared in advance; if you do this, cook the prawns and bacon just before serving, spoon over the salad and serve with hot herb and garlic bread.

Serves 8

INGREDIENTS
225 g/8 oz large, cooked, shelled prawns
225 g/8 oz smoked streaky bacon, chopped
mixed lettuce leaves
30 ml/2 tbsp snipped fresh chives

FOR THE LEMON AND CHILLI MARINADE
1 garlic clove, crushed
finely grated rind of 1 lemon
15 ml/1 tbsp lemon juice
60 ml/4 tbsp olive oil
¼ tsp chilli paste, or a large pinch dried ground chilli
15 ml/1 tbsp light soy sauce
salt and freshly ground black pepper

prawns
chilli paste
lettuce leaves
chives
soy sauce
lemon
garlic
bacon

1 In a glass bowl, mix the prawns with the garlic, lemon rind and juice, 45 ml/ 3 tbsp of oil, the chilli paste and soy sauce. Season with salt and pepper. Cover with clear film and leave to marinate for at least one hour.

2 Gently cook the bacon in the remaining oil until crisp. Drain on a kitchen towel.

3 Wash and dry the lettuce, tear the leaves into bite-sized pieces and arrange them in individual bowls or on plates.

4 Just before serving, put the prawns with their marinade into a large frying-pan, bring to the boil, add the bacon and cook for one minute. Spoon over the salad and sprinkle with snipped chives. Serve immediately.

Smoked Salmon Salad

To save time, prepare all the ingredients in advance and assemble them on the plates just before serving. The dressing can be made the day before and kept in the fridge.

Serves 8

INGREDIENTS
4 thin slices white bread
oil, for frying
paprika, for dusting
mixed lettuce leaves
25 g/1 oz Parmesan cheese
225 g/8 oz smoked salmon or trout,
    thinly sliced
1 lemon

FOR THE VINAIGRETTE DRESSING
90 ml/6 tbsp olive oil
30 ml/2 tbsp red wine vinegar
1 garlic clove, crushed
5 ml/1 tsp Dijon mustard
5 ml/1 tsp runny honey
15 ml/1 tbsp chopped fresh parsley
2.5 ml/½ tsp fresh thyme
10 ml/2 tsp capers, chopped
salt and freshly ground black pepper

lettuce leaves

lemon

paprika

bread

smoked salmon

1 First make the dressing. Put all the ingredients into a screw-top jar and shake the jar well to emulsify the dressing. Season to taste.

2 With a small star-shaped cutter, stamp out as many shapes from the slices of bread as possible. Heat 2.5 cm/1 in oil in a shallow frying-pan until the oil is almost smoking (test it with a cube of bread, it should sizzle on the surface and brown within 30 seconds). Fry the croûtons, in small batches, until golden brown all over. Remove the croûtons with a slotted spoon and let them drain on kitchen paper. Dust with paprika and leave to cool.

3 Wash the lettuce, dry the leaves and tear them into small bite-sized pieces. Wrap in a clean, damp tea towel and keep the lettuce in the fridge until ready to serve.

4 Cut the Parmesan cheese into wafer-thin flakes with a vegetable peeler. Put into a dish and cover with clear film.

5 Cut the salmon or trout into 1 cm/½ in strips no more than 5 cm/2 in long. Cut the lemon into eight thin wedges.

6 To assemble the salad, arrange the lettuce on individual plates, scatter over the Parmesan flakes and arrange the salmon strips on top. Shake the dressing vigorously to emulsify it again and spoon a little over each salad. Scatter over the croûtons, place a lemon wedge on the side of each plate and serve immediately.

Roquefort Tartlets

These can be made in shallow tartlet tins to serve hot as a first course. You could also make them in tiny cocktail tins, to serve warm as bite-sized snacks with a drink before a meal.

Makes 12

INGREDIENTS
175 g/6 oz/1½ cup plain flour
large pinch of salt
115 g/4 oz/½ cup butter
1 egg yolk
30 ml/2 tbsp cold water

FOR THE FILLING
15 g/½ oz/1 tbsp butter
15 g/½ oz/1 tbsp flour
150 ml/¼ pint/⅔ cup milk
115 g/4 oz Roquefort cheese, crumbled
150 ml/¼ pint/⅔ cup double cream
2.5 ml/½ tsp dried mixed herbs
3 egg yolks
salt and freshly ground black pepper

flour

milk

Roquefort

butter

eggs

1 To make the pastry, sift the flour and salt into a bowl and rub the butter into the flour until it resembles breadcrumbs. Mix the egg yolk with the water and stir into the flour to make a soft dough. Knead until smooth, wrap in clear film and chill for 30 minutes. (You can also make the dough in a food processor.)

2 Melt the butter, stir in the flour and then the milk. Boil to thicken, stirring continuously. Off the heat beat in the cheese and season. Cool. Bring the cream and herbs to the boil. Reduce to 30 ml/2 tbsp. Beat into the sauce with the eggs.

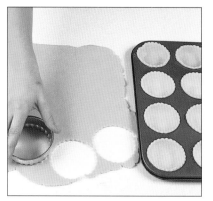

3 Preheat the oven to 190°C/375°F/ Gas 5. On a lightly floured work surface, roll out the pastry 3mm/⅛ in thick. Stamp out rounds with a fluted cutter and use to line your chosen tartlet tins.

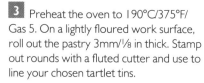

4 Divide the filling between the tartlets; they should be filled only two-thirds full. Stamp out smaller fluted rounds or star shapes for the tops and lay on top of each tartlet. Bake for 20–25 minutes, or until puffed and golden brown.

Potted Stilton with Herbs and Melba Toast

Make this the day before and serve it in small ramekin dishes with the crisp Melba toast, as a snack or first course. The Melba toast will keep in an airtight container for a day or two.

Serves 8

INGREDIENTS
225 g/8 oz blue Stilton or other
   blue cheese
115 g/4 oz cream cheese
15 ml/1 tbsp port
15 ml/1 tbsp chopped fresh parsley
15 ml/1 tbsp snipped fresh chives,
   plus extra to garnish
50 g/2 oz/½ cup finely chopped
   walnuts
salt and freshly ground black pepper

FOR THE MELBA TOAST
12 thin slices white bread

Stilton

walnuts   bread

parsley

cream cheese

chives

1 Put the Stilton, cream cheese and port into a bowl or food processor and beat until smooth.

2 Stir in the remaining ingredients and season with salt and pepper to taste.

3 Spoon into individual ramekin dishes and level the tops. Cover with clear film and chill until firm. Sprinkle with snipped chives before serving. To make the melba toast, preheat the oven to 180°C/350°F/Gas 4. Toast the bread on both sides.

4 While the toast is still hot, cut off the crusts, and cut each slice horizontally in two. While the bread is still warm, place it in a single layer on baking trays and bake for 10–15 minutes, until golden brown and crisp. Continue with the remaining slices in the same way. Serve warm with the potted Stilton.

Baked Gammon with Cumberland Sauce

Serve this delicious cooked meat and sauce either hot or cold. The gammon must be soaked overnight before cooking to remove any strong salty flavour resulting from the curing process.

Serves 8–10

INGREDIENTS
2.25 kg/5 lb smoked or unsmoked
    gammon joint
1 onion
1 carrot
1 celery stick
bouquet garni sachet
6 peppercorns

FOR THE GLAZE
whole cloves
2 oz/50 g/4 tbsp soft light brown or
    demerara sugar
30 ml/2 tbsp golden syrup
5 ml/1 tsp English mustard powder

FOR THE CUMBERLAND SAUCE
juice and shredded rind of 1 orange
30 ml/2 tbsp lemon juice
120 ml/4 fl oz/½ cup port or red wine
60 ml/4 tbsp redcurrant jelly

1 Soak the gammon overnight in a cool place in plenty of cold water to cover. Discard this water. Put the joint into a large pan and cover it again with more cold water. Bring the water to the boil slowly and skim any scum from the surface with a slotted spoon.

2 Add the vegetables and seasonings, cover and simmer very gently for 2 hours. (The meat can also be cooked in the oven at 180°C/350°F/Gas 4. Allow 30 minutes per 450 g/1 lb.)

3 Leave the meat to cool in the liquid for 30 minutes. Then remove it from the liquid and strip off the skin neatly with the help of a knife (use rubber gloves if the gammon is too hot to handle).

4 Score the fat in diamonds with a sharp knife and stick a clove in the centre of each diamond.

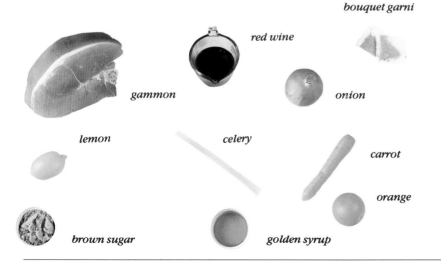

bouquet garni

red wine

gammon

onion

lemon

celery

carrot

orange

brown sugar

golden syrup

5 Preheat the oven to 180°C/350°F/ Gas 4. Put the sugar, golden syrup and mustard powder in a small pan and heat gently to melt them. Place the gammon in a roasting tin and spoon over the glaze. Bake it until golden brown, about 20 minutes. Put it under a hot grill, if necessary, to get a good colour. Allow to stand in a warm place for 15 minutes before carving (this allows the flesh to relax and makes carving much easier).

6 For the sauce, put the orange and lemon juice into a pan with the port and redcurrant jelly, and heat gently to melt the jelly. Pour boiling water on to the orange rind, drain, and add to the sauce. Cook gently for 2 minutes. Serve the sauce hot, in a sauce boat.

Roast Turkey

Serve with stuffing balls, bacon rolls, roast potatoes, Brussels sprouts and gravy.

Serves 8

INGREDIENTS
4.5 kg/10 lb oven-ready turkey, with giblets (thawed overnight if frozen)
1 large onion, peeled and stuck with 6 whole cloves
50 g/2 oz/4 tbsp butter, softened
10 chipolata sausages
salt and freshly ground black pepper

FOR THE STUFFING
225 g/8 oz rindless, streaky bacon, chopped
1 large onion, finely chopped
450 g/1 lb pork sausagemeat
25 g/1 oz/⅓ cup rolled oats
30 ml/2 tbsp chopped fresh parsley
10 ml/2 tsp dried mixed herbs
1 large egg, beaten
115 g/4 oz dried apricots, finely chopped

FOR THE GRAVY
25 g/1 oz/2 tbsp plain flour
450 ml/¾ pint/1⅞ cups giblet stock

bacon

turkey

onion

parsley

apricots   oats

1 Preheat the oven to 200°C/400°F/Gas 6. Adjust the oven shelves to allow for the size of the turkey. For the stuffing, cook the bacon and onion gently in a pan until the bacon is crisp and the onion tender. Transfer to a large bowl and mix in all the remaining stuffing ingredients. Season well with salt and pepper.

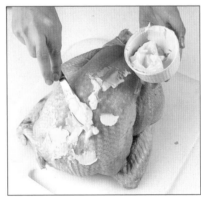

4 Spread the turkey with the butter and season it with salt and pepper. Cover it loosely with foil and cook it for 30 minutes. Baste the turkey with the pan juices. Then lower the oven temperature to 180°C/350°F/Gas 4 and cook for the remainder of the calculated time (about 3½ hours for a 4.5 kg/10 lb bird). Baste it every 30 minutes or so.

2 Stuff the neck-end of the turkey only, tuck the flap of skin under and secure it with a small skewer or stitch it with thread (do not over-stuff the turkey or the skin will burst during cooking). Reserve any remaining stuffing.

3 Put the whole onion studded with cloves in the body cavity of the turkey and tie the legs together. Weigh the stuffed bird and calculate the cooking time; allow 15 minutes per 450 g/1 lb plus 15 minutes over. Place the turkey in a large roasting tin.

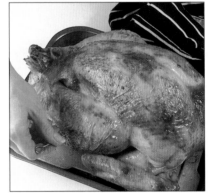

5 With wet hands, shape the remaining stuffing into small balls or pack it into a greased ovenproof dish. Cook in the oven for 20 minutes, or until golden brown and crisp. About 20 minutes before the end of cooking put the chipolata sausages into an ovenproof dish and put them in the oven. Remove the foil from the turkey for the last hour of cooking and baste it. The turkey is cooked if the juices run clear when the thickest part of the thigh has been pierced with a skewer.

6 Transfer the turkey to a serving plate, cover it with foil and let it stand for 15 minutes before carving. To make the gravy, spoon off the fat from the roasting pan, leaving the meat juices. Blend in the flour and cook for 2 minutes. Gradually stir in the stock and bring to the boil. Check the seasoning and pour into a sauce boat. Remove the skewer or string and pour any juices into the gravy. To serve, surround the turkey with chipolata sausages, bacon rolls and stuffing balls.

Roast Duck with Orange

Most of the meat on a duck is on the breast. It is easier to cut the whole breast off each side of the carcass and slice it thinly on a board. The ducks can be cooked the day before, sliced and reheated in some of the gravy. The remaining gravy, with the orange segments, can be reheated gently just before serving.

Serves 8

INGREDIENTS
4 oranges, segmented, with rind and
  juice reserved
2 × 2.25 kg/5 lb oven-ready ducks,
  with giblets
salt and freshly ground black pepper

FOR THE SAUCE
30 ml/2 tbsp flour
300 ml/½ pint/1¼ cups giblet stock
150 ml/¼ pint/⅔ cup port or red
  wine
15 ml/1 tbsp redcurrant jelly

giblet stock

port

duck

oranges

flour

1 Preheat the oven to 180°C/350°F/Gas 4. Tie the orange rind with string and place it inside the cavities of the ducks.

2 Place the ducks on a rack in a roasting tin, season and cook for 30 minutes per 450 g/1 lb (about 2½ hours), until the flesh is tender and the juices run clear. Pour off the fat into a bowl half-way through the cooking time.

3 Transfer the ducks to a carving board and remove the orange rind from the cavities. To make the sauce, remove any fat from the roasting tin, leaving the sediment and juices behind. Sprinkle in the flour and cook gently for 2 minutes. Blend in the rest of the ingredients and reserved orange rind, roughly chopped. Bring to the boil and simmer for 10 minutes; then strain into a pan, and add the orange segments, with their juice.

4 To carve the ducks, remove the legs and wings, cutting through the joints. Cut the two end joints off the wings and discard them. Cut the breast-meat off the carcass in one piece and slice it thinly. Arrange the slices on a warm serving plate with the legs and the wing joints. Spoon over some of the hot sauce and serve the rest separately in a sauce boat.

Spiced Lamb with Fruit Pilaf

This wonderfully rich and spicy dish is excellent for a New Year's Eve party. It can be made the day before and reheated gently in the oven before serving. It freezes well too.

Serves 8

INGREDIENTS
45 ml/3 tbsp olive oil
1.2 kg/2½ lb fillet-end boneless leg of
 lamb, cut into 4 cm/1½ in cubes
2 large onions, chopped
2–3 garlic cloves, crushed
30 ml/2 tbsp flour
5 ml/1 tsp ground cumin
5 ml/1 tsp ground coriander
2.5 ml/½ tsp ground allspice
45 ml/3 tbsp tomato purée
300 ml/½ pint/1¼ cups lamb stock
150 ml/¼ pint/⅔ cup red wine
salt and freshly ground black pepper

FOR THE FRUIT PILAF
40 g/1½ oz/3 tbsp butter
1 onion, chopped
5 ml/1 tsp ground turmeric
350 g/12 oz/1¾ cups long-grain rice
750 ml/1¼ pints/3⅔ cups stock
115 g/4 oz no-soak apricots, chopped
115 g/4 oz/⅔ cup pistachio nuts

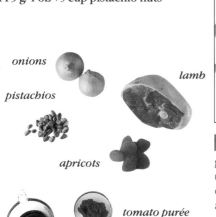

onions

lamb

pistachios

apricots

tomato purée

rice

red wine

1 Preheat the oven to 180°C/350°F/ Gas 4. Heat the oil in a casserole and brown the meat a few pieces at a time. Remove the lamb after it has browned and keep it warm.

2 Lower the heat, add the onions and garlic to the casserole and cook gently until tender, about 5 minutes, stirring occasionally. Stir in the flour and spices and cook slowly for 3–4 minutes.

3 Stir in the tomato purée, stock and wine, blending them in gradually until the sauce is smooth. Bring to the boil to thicken and season. Replace the meat, cover the casserole and cook it in the preheated oven for 45–55 minutes, or until the lamb is tender. (Cook for half the time if you are cooking ahead to reheat the next day.)

4 To make the pilaf, melt the butter and cook the onion until tender. Stir in the turmeric and rice and cook for 2 minutes. Then add the stock and season. Bring to the boil, cover and cook in the oven for 20–30 minutes, or until the rice is tender and all the liquid has been absorbed. Stir in the apricots and pistachio nuts, cover and allow to stand for 10–15 minutes.

Roast Goose with Caramelized Apples and Port and Orange Gravy

Choose a young goose with a pliable breast bone.

Serves 8

INGREDIENTS

4.5–5.5 kg/10–12 lb goose, with
    giblets
salt and freshly ground black pepper

FOR THE APPLE AND NUT STUFFING

225 g/8 oz/2 cups prunes
150 ml/¼ pint/⅔ cup port or
    red wine
675 g/1½ lb cooking apples, peeled,
    cored and cubed
1 large onion, chopped
4 celery sticks, sliced
15 ml/1 tbsp mixed dried herbs
finely grated rind of 1 orange
goose liver, chopped
450 g/1 lb pork sausagemeat
115 g/4 oz/1 cup chopped pecans or
    walnuts
2 eggs

FOR THE CARAMELIZED APPLES

50 g/2 oz/4 tbsp butter
60 ml/4 tbsp redcurrant jelly
30 ml/2 tbsp red wine vinegar
8 small dessert apples, peeled and
    cored

FOR THE GRAVY

30 ml/2 tbsp plain flour
600 ml/1 pint/2½ cups giblet stock
juice of 1 orange

apples

goose

prunes

orange

onion *eggs*

sausagemeat

1 The day before you want to cook the goose, soak the prunes in the port or red wine. Then stone each one and cut it into four pieces, reserving the port.

2 Mix with all the remaining stuffing ingredients and season well. Moisten with half the reserved port.

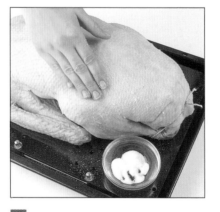

3 Preheat the oven to 200°C/400°F/ Gas 6. Stuff the neck-end of the goose, tucking the flap of skin under and securing it with a small skewer. Remove the excess fat from the cavity and pack it with the stuffing. Tie the legs together to hold them in place.

4 Weigh the stuffed goose and calculate the cooking time: allow 15 minutes per 450 g/1 lb. Put the bird on a rack in a roasting tin and rub the skin with salt. You may prick the skin all over to help the fat run out. Roast it for 30 minutes, then reduce the heat to 180°C/ 350°F/Gas 4 and roast for the remaining cooking time. Pour off any fat produced during cooking into a bowl. The goose is cooked if the juices run clear when the thickest part of the thigh has been pierced with a skewer. Pour a little cold water over the breast to crisp the skin.

5 Meanwhile, prepare the apples. Melt the butter, redcurrant jelly and vinegar in a small roasting tin or a shallow ovenproof dish. Put in the apples, baste them well and cook in the oven for 15–20 minutes. Baste the apples half-way through the cooking time. Do not overcook them or they will collapse.

6 Lift the goose on to a serving dish and let it stand for 15 minutes before carving. Pour off the excess fat from the roasting tin, leaving any sediment in the bottom. Stir in the flour, cook gently until golden brown, and then blend in the stock. Bring to the boil, add the remaining reserved port, orange juice and seasoning. Simmer for 2–3 minutes. Strain into a gravy boat. Surround the goose with the caramelized apples and spoon over the redcurrant glaze.

Tenderloin of Pork Wrapped in Bacon

This easy-to-carve 'joint' is served with an onion and prune gravy.

Serves 8

INGREDIENTS

3 large pork fillets, weighing about
   1.2 kg/2½ lb in total
225 g/8 oz rindless streaky bacon
25 g/1 oz/2 tbsp butter
150 ml/¼ pint/⅔ cup red wine

FOR THE PRUNE STUFFING

25 g/1 oz/2 tbsp butter
1 onion, very finely chopped
115 g/4 oz mushrooms, very finely
   chopped
4 no-soak prunes, stoned and chopped
10 ml/2 tsp dried mixed herbs
115 g/4 oz/2 cups fresh white
   breadcrumbs
1 egg
salt and freshly ground black pepper

TO FINISH

16 no-soak prunes
150 ml/¼ pint/⅔ cup red wine
16 pickling onions
30 ml/2 tbsp plain flour
300 ml/½ pint/1¼ cups
   chicken stock

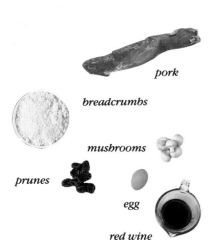

pork

breadcrumbs

mushrooms

prunes

egg

red wine

1 Preheat the oven to 180°C/350°F/Gas 4. Trim the fillets, removing any sinew and fat. Cut each fillet lengthways, three-quarters of the way through, open them out and flatten.

2 For the stuffing, melt the butter and cook the onion until tender, add the mushrooms and cook for 5 minutes. Transfer to a bowl and mix in the remaining stuffing ingredients. Spread the stuffing over two of the fillets and sandwich together with the third fillet.

3 Stretch each rasher of bacon with the back of a large knife.

4 Lay the rashers overlapping across the meat. Cut lengths of string and lay them at 2 cm/¾ in intervals over the bacon. Cover with a piece of foil to hold in place, and roll the 'joint' over. Fold the bacon rashers over the meat and tie the string to secure them in place. Roll the 'joint' back on to the bacon joins and remove the foil.

5 Place in a roasting tin and spread the butter over the 'joint'. Pour round the wine and cook for 1¼ hours, basting occasionally with the liquid in the roasting tin, until evenly browned. Simmer the remaining prunes in the red wine until tender. Boil the onions in salted water for 10 minutes, or until just tender. Drain and add to the prunes.

6 Transfer the pork to a serving plate, remove the string, cover loosely with foil and leave to stand for 10–15 minutes, before slicing. Remove any fat from the roasting tin, add the flour to the sediment and juices and cook gently for 2–3 minutes. Then blend in the stock, bring to the boil and simmer for 5 minutes. Adjust the seasoning to taste. Strain the gravy on to the prunes and onions, reheat and serve in a sauce boat with a ladle.

Individual Beef Wellingtons

The sauce can be made the day before and reheated just before serving. The Wellingtons can be made several hours before cooking, as long as the meat is quite cold before you wrap it in pastry. Keep them in the refrigerator before cooking.

Serves 8

INGREDIENTS

30 ml/2 tbsp olive oil
8 beef fillet steaks, cut 2.5 cm/1 in thick, weighing about 115 g/ 4 oz each
900 g/2 lb puff pastry, thawed if frozen
225 g/8 oz smooth garlic liver sausage or pâté
30 ml/2 tbsp chopped fresh parsley
30 ml/2 tbsp snipped fresh chives
1 egg, beaten with 15 ml/1 tbsp water

FOR THE SAUCE

25 g/1 oz/2 tbsp butter
1 onion, finely chopped
115 g/4 oz mushrooms, finely chopped
30 ml/2 tbsp plain flour
2.5 ml/½ tsp tomato purée
2.5 ml/½ tsp caster sugar
150 ml/¼ pint/⅔ cup red wine
300 ml/½ pint/1¼ cups beef stock
salt and freshly ground black pepper

1 Heat the oil in a large frying-pan and quickly brown the steaks on both sides. Transfer to a plate and leave to cool. Preheat the oven to 200°C/400°F/Gas 6.

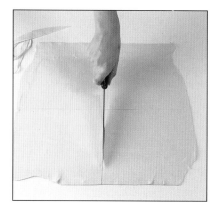

2 Divide the pastry in two equal halves. On a lightly floured work surface, roll each piece out thinly and trim to a 40 cm/16 in square. Cut into four 20 cm/ 8 in squares. (Save the trimmings for the decoration.)

3 Mix the liver sausage or pâté with the herbs. Place a cold fillet steak on each piece of pastry and divide the sausage or pâté between each. Spread evenly over the top and sides.

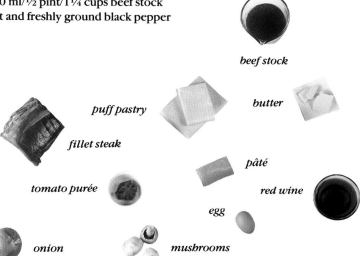

beef stock

puff pastry

butter

fillet steak

pâté

tomato purée

red wine

egg

onion

mushrooms

4 Brush the pastry with beaten egg and fold the sides over like a parcel. Pinch the edges to seal.

5 Place on baking trays, seam-side down and decorate the tops with a lattice cut from the trimmings. When ready to cook them, brush the pastry all over with beaten egg and bake for 25 minutes, or until golden brown. (Do not brush the Wellingtons with egg until just before baking, as the egg dries in the fridge.)

6 To make the sauce, heat the butter and cook the onion until tender. Add the mushrooms and cook for 5 minutes, stirring occasionally. Stir in the flour, tomato purée and sugar and blend in the red wine and stock. Bring to the boil and simmer for 10 minutes. Season to taste, then strain into a gravy boat and serve separately.

Filo Vegetable Pie

This stunning pie makes a delicious main course for vegetarians or is an excellent accompaniment to cold sliced turkey or other meat dishes.

Serves 6–8

INGREDIENTS
225 g/8 oz leeks
165 g/5½ oz/11 tbsp butter
225 g/8 oz carrots, cubed
225 g/8 oz mushrooms, sliced
225 g/8 oz Brussels sprouts, quartered
2 garlic cloves, crushed
115 g/4 oz cream cheese
115 g/4 oz Roquefort or Stilton cheese
150 ml/¼ pint/⅔ cup double cream
2 eggs, beaten
225 g/8 oz cooking apples
225 g/8 oz/1 cup cashew nuts or pine nuts, toasted
350 g/12 oz frozen filo pastry, defrosted
salt and freshly ground black pepper

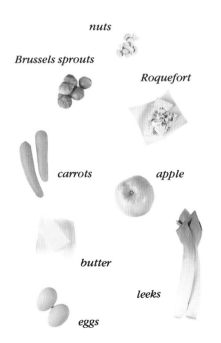

nuts
Brussels sprouts
Roquefort
carrots
apple
butter
leeks
eggs

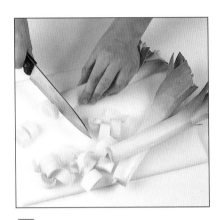

1 Preheat the oven to 180°C/350°F/ Gas 4. Cut the leeks in half through the root and wash them to remove any soil, separating the layers slightly to check they are clean. Slice into 1 cm/½ in pieces, drain and dry on kitchen paper.

2 Heat 40 g/1½ oz/3 tbsp of the butter in a large pan and cook the leeks and carrots covered over a medium heat for 5 minutes. Add the mushrooms, sprouts and garlic and cook for another 2 minutes. Turn the vegetables into a bowl and let them cool.

3 Whisk the cream cheese and blue cheese, cream, eggs and seasoning together in a bowl. Pour them over the vegetables. Peel and core the apples and cut into 1 cm/½ in cubes. Add them to the vegetables, with the toasted nuts.

4 Melt the remaining butter. Brush the inside of a 23 cm/9 in loose-based springform cake tin with melted butter. Brush two-thirds of the filo pastry sheets with butter, one at a time and use them to line the base and sides of the tin, overlapping the layers so that there are no gaps.

5 Spoon in the vegetable mixture and fold over the excess filo pastry to cover the filling.

6 Brush the remaining filo sheets with butter and cut them into 2.5 cm/1 in strips. Cover the top of the pie with these strips, arranging them in a rough mound. Bake for 35–45 minutes until golden brown all over. Allow to stand for 5 minutes, and then remove the cake tin and transfer to a serving plate.

Cheese and Spinach Flan

This flan freezes well and can be reheated. It's an excellent addition to a festive buffet party and is popular with vegetarians too. If you don't have a lattice cutter, cut the pastry into strips and make a lattice following the instructions given for the De Luxe Mincemeat Tart.

Serves 8

INGREDIENTS
115 g/4 oz/½ cup butter
225 g/8 oz/2 cups plain flour
2.5 ml/½ tsp English mustard powder
2.5 ml/½ tsp paprika
large pinch of salt
115 g/4 oz Cheddar cheese, finely
   grated
45–60 ml/3–4 tbsp cold water
1 egg, beaten, to glaze

FOR THE FILLING
450 g/1 lb frozen spinach
1 onion, chopped
pinch of grated nutmeg
225 g/8 oz cottage cheese
2 large eggs
50 g/2 oz Parmesan cheese, grated
150 ml/¼ pint/⅔ cup single cream
salt and freshly ground black pepper

eggs
flour
Cheddar
butter
cream
cottage cheese
spinach

1 Rub the butter into the flour until it resembles fine breadcrumbs. Rub in the next four ingredients. Bind to a dough with the cold water. Knead until smooth, wrap and chill for 30 minutes.

2 Put the spinach and onion in a pan, cover, and cook slowly. Increase the heat to drive off any water. Season with salt, pepper and nutmeg. Turn the spinach into a bowl, cool slightly. Add the remaining filling ingredients.

3 Preheat the oven to 200°C/400°F/Gas 6. Put a baking tray in the oven to preheat. Cut one-third off the pastry for the lid. On a lightly floured surface, roll out the remaining pastry and use it to line a 23 cm/9 in loose-based flan tin. Press the pastry well into the edges and make a narrow lip around the top edge. Remove the excess pastry with a rolling pin. Pour the filling into the flan case.

4 Roll out the remaining pastry and cut it with a lattice pastry cutter. Carefully open the lattice. With the help of a rolling pin, lay it over the flan. Brush the joins with egg glaze. Press the edges together and trim off the excess pastry. Brush the pastry lattice with egg glaze and bake on the hot baking tray for 35–40 minutes, or until golden brown. Serve hot or cold.

Gratin Dauphinois

This dish can be made and baked in advance; reheat it in the oven for 20–30 minutes. This is a good alternative to roast potatoes and it needs no last-minute attention.

Serves 8

INGREDIENTS
butter, for greasing
1.75 kg/3½ lb potatoes
2–3 garlic cloves, crushed
2.5 ml/½ tsp grated nutmeg
115 g/4 oz Cheddar cheese, grated
600 ml/1 pint/2½ cups milk
300 ml/½ pint/1¼ cups single cream
2 large eggs, beaten
salt and freshly ground black pepper

cream

potatoes

Cheddar

eggs

nutmeg

garlic

1 Preheat the oven to 180°C/350°F/ Gas 4. Butter a 2.4 litre/4 pint/10 cup shallow ovenproof dish. Peel the potatoes and slice them thinly.

2 Layer the potatoes in the dish, with the garlic, nutmeg and two-thirds of the grated cheese and season well.

3 Whisk the milk, cream and eggs together and pour them over the potatoes, making sure the liquid goes all the way to the bottom of the dish.

4 Scatter the remaining cheese on top and bake for 45–50 minutes, or until golden brown. Test the potatoes with a sharp knife; they should be very tender.

Cheese, Rice and Vegetable Strudel

Based on a traditional Russian dish called 'Koulibiac', this makes a perfect vegetarian main course or an unusual accompaniment to cold leftover turkey or sliced ham.

Serves 8

INGREDIENTS
175 g/6 oz/⅞ cup long-grain rice
25 g/1 oz/2 tbsp butter
1–2 leeks, thinly sliced
350 g/12 oz mushrooms, sliced
225 g/8 oz Gruyère or Cheddar
  cheese, grated
225 g/8 oz feta cheese, cubed
30 ml/2 tbsp currants
50 g/2 oz/½ cup chopped almonds or
  hazelnuts, toasted
30 ml/2 tbsp chopped fresh parsley
275 g/10 oz packet frozen filo pastry,
  thawed
30 ml/2 tbsp olive oil
salt and freshly ground black pepper

feta

leek

rice

parsley

filo
pastry

almonds

mushrooms

currants

1 Cook the rice in boiling, salted water for 10–12 minutes, until tender. Drain, rinse under cold running water and set aside. Melt the butter and cook the leeks and mushrooms for 5 minutes. Transfer to a bowl to cool.

2 Add the well-drained rice, the cheeses, currants, toasted nuts, parsley and season to taste (be careful with the salt as the feta cheese is very salty).

3 Preheat the oven to 190°C/375°F/ Gas 5. Unwrap the filo pastry. Cover it with a piece of clear film and a damp cloth while you work. Lay a sheet of filo pastry on a large piece of greaseproof paper and brush it with oil. Lay a second sheet, overlapping the first by 2.5 cm/1 in. Put another sheet with its long side running at right angles to the long sides of the first two. Lay a fourth sheet in the same way, overlapping by 2.5 cm/1 in. Continue in this way, alternating the layers of two sheets so that the join between the two sheets runs in the opposite direction for each layer.

4 Place the filling along the centre of the pastry and shape it neatly with your hands into a rectangle approximately 10 × 30 cm/4 × 12 in.

5 Fold the pastry over the filling and roll it over, with the help of the greaseproof paper, so that the join is hidden underneath.

6 Lift the strudel on to a greased baking tray and tuck the edges under, so that the filling does not escape during cooking. Brush with oil and bake for 30–40 minutes, until golden and crisp. Let the strudel stand for 5 minutes before cutting.

Vegetable Gougère

This makes a light vegetarian supper, or a main meal served with a salad and baked potatoes.

Serves 4

INGREDIENTS
50 g/2 oz/4 tbsp butter
150 ml/¼ pint/⅔ cup water
65 g/2½ oz/⅔ cup plain flour
2 eggs, beaten
¼ tsp English mustard
50 g/2 oz Cheddar or Gruyère cheese, cubed
salt and freshly ground black pepper
10 ml/2 tsp chopped fresh parsley, to garnish

FOR THE FILLING
25 g/1 oz/2 tbsp butter
1 onion, sliced
1 garlic clove, crushed
225 g/8 oz mushrooms, sliced
15 ml/1 tbsp plain flour
1 × 400 g/14 oz can tomatoes
5 ml/1 tsp caster sugar
225 g/8 oz courgettes, sliced thickly

FOR THE TOPPING
15 ml/1 tbsp grated Parmesan cheese
15 ml/1 tbsp breadcrumbs, toasted

tomatoes   mushrooms

courgettes

butter

flour

1 Preheat the oven to 200°C/400°F/ Gas 6. To make the choux pastry, melt the butter in a pan, add the water and bring to the boil. As soon as the liquid is boiling, draw the pan off the heat and beat in the flour all at once, until a smooth paste is formed. Turn into a large bowl and allow to cool slightly.

2 With an electric whisk, beat the eggs gradually into the paste until the mixture is glossy but firm. Season with salt, pepper and mustard powder. Fold in the cheese. Set aside.

3 To make the filling, melt the butter in a pan and cook the onion gently until tender. Add the garlic and mushrooms and cook for 2–3 minutes. Stir in the flour and the tomatoes and their juice. Bring to the boil, stirring, to thicken. Season with salt, pepper and sugar to taste. Lastly add the sliced courgettes.

4 Butter a 1.2 litre/2 pint/5 cup ovenproof dish. Spoon the choux pastry in rough mounds around the sides of the dish and turn the filling into the centre. Sprinkle the Parmesan cheese and breadcrumbs on top of the filling. Bake for 35–40 minutes, until the pastry is well risen and golden brown. Sprinkle with chopped parsley and serve hot.

Vegetable Crumble with Anchovies

The anchovies may be left out of this dish in order that vegetarians can enjoy it, but they give the vegetables a delicious flavour. Serve as an accompaniment to sliced turkey or ham.

Serves 8

INGREDIENTS
450 g/1 lb potatoes
225 g/8 oz leeks
25 g/1 oz/2 tbsp butter
450 g/1 lb carrots, chopped
2 garlic cloves, crushed
225 g/8 oz mushrooms, sliced
450 g/1 lb Brussels sprouts, sliced
1 × 40 g/1½ oz can anchovies,
   drained
salt and freshly ground black pepper

FOR THE CHEESE CRUMBLE
50 g/2 oz/4 tbsp plain flour
50 g/2 oz/4 tbsp butter
50 g/2 oz/1 cup fresh breadcrumbs
50 g/2 oz Cheddar cheese, grated
30 ml/2 tbsp chopped fresh parsley
5 ml/1 tsp English mustard powder

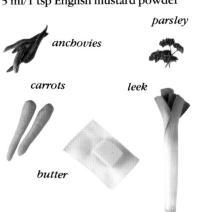

parsley

anchovies

carrots   *leek*

butter

mushrooms

potato

1 Peel and halve the potatoes and parboil them in salted water until just tender. Drain and cool. Cut the leeks in half lengthways and wash them thoroughly to remove any soil. Drain and slice in 1 cm/½ in pieces.

2 Melt the butter and cook the leeks and carrots for 2–3 minutes. Add the garlic and mushrooms and cook for a further 3 minutes. Add the sprouts. Season with pepper. Transfer to a 2.5 litre/4 pint/10 cup ovenproof dish.

3 Preheat the oven to 200°C/400°F/ Gas 6. Chop the anchovies and scatter them over the vegetables. Slice the potatoes and arrange them on top.

4 To make the crumble, sift the flour into a bowl and rub in the butter or process in a food processor. Add the breadcrumbs and mix in the remaining ingredients. Spoon over the vegetables and bake for 20–30 minutes.

Vegetable Gnocchi

This delicious vegetarian main course can be assembled well ahead of time and cooked in the oven without any last-minute preparation.

Serves 8

INGREDIENTS
450 g/1 lb frozen spinach
15 g/½ oz/1 tbsp butter
¼ tsp grated nutmeg
225 g/8 oz ricotta or curd cheese
115 g/4 oz Parmesan cheese, grated
2 eggs, beaten
115 g/4 oz/1 cup plain flour
50 g/2 oz Cheddar cheese, grated
salt and freshly ground black pepper

FOR THE SAUCE
50 g/2 oz/4 tbsp butter
50 g/2 oz/4 tbsp flour
600 ml/1 pint/2½ cups milk

FOR THE VEGETABLE LAYER
25 g/1 oz/2 tbsp butter
2 leeks or onions, sliced
4 carrots, sliced
4 celery sticks, sliced
4 courgettes, sliced

1 Put the spinach in a large pan with the butter and heat gently to defrost it. Then increase the heat to drive off any moisture. Season with salt, pepper and nutmeg. Turn into a bowl and mix in the ricotta or curd cheese, Parmesan cheese, eggs and flour. Beat until smooth.

2 Shape the mixture into ovals with two dessertspoons and place them on a lightly floured tray. Place in the refrigerator for 30 minutes.

3 Have a large shallow pan of boiling, salted water ready. Cook the gnocchi in two batches, for about 5 minutes (the water should simmer gently and not boil). As soon as the gnocchi rise to the surface, remove them with a slotted spoon and let them drain on a clean tea towel.

4 Preheat the oven to 180°C/350°F/ Gas 4. For the sauce, melt the butter in a pan, add the flour and blend in the milk. Bring to the boil to thicken and season to taste.

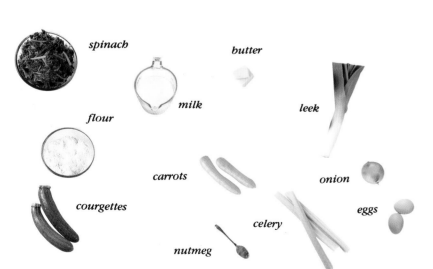

spinach

butter

milk

flour

leek

carrots

onion

courgettes

celery

eggs

nutmeg

5 For the vegetable layer, melt the butter and cook the leeks, carrots and celery until tender, about 5 minutes. Add the courgettes, season with salt and pepper and stir to mix. Turn into a 2.4 litre/4 pint/10 cup ovenproof dish.

6 Place the drained gnocchi on top, spoon over the sauce and sprinkle with grated cheese. Bake for 30 minutes, until golden brown. Grill if necessary.

Brussels Sprouts with Chestnuts and Carrots

Be sure to allow plenty of time to peel the chestnuts; they are very fiddly but well worth the effort.

Serves 8

INGREDIENTS
450 g/1 lb fresh chestnuts
450 ml/¾ pint/1⅞ cups vegetable
    stock
450 g/1 lb Brussels sprouts
450 g/1 lb carrots
25 g/1 oz/2 tbsp butter
salt and freshly ground black pepper

carrots

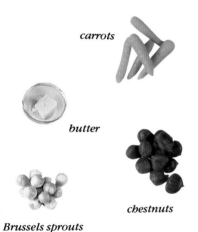

butter

chestnuts

Brussels sprouts

1 Using a sharp knife, peel the raw chestnuts, leaving the brown papery skins intact. Bring a small pan of water to the boil, drop a handful of chestnuts into the water for a few minutes, and remove with a slotted spoon. The brown papery skins will slip off easily.

2 Put the peeled chestnuts in a pan with the stock. Cover the pan and bring to the boil. Simmer for 5–10 minutes, until tender. Drain.

3 Remove the outer leaves from the sprouts, if necessary, and trim the stalks level. Cook in a pan of boiling, salted water for about 5 minutes, or until just tender. Drain and rinse under cold running water to stop the cooking.

4 Peel the carrots and cut them in 1 cm/½ in diagonal slices. Put them in a pan with cold water to cover, bring to the boil and simmer until just tender, 5–6 minutes. Drain and rinse under cold running water. Melt the butter in a heavy-based pan, add the chestnuts, sprouts and carrots and season with salt and pepper. Cover with a lid and reheat, occasionally stirring the vegetables in the pan.

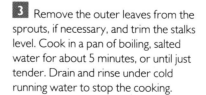

Sweet and Sour Red Cabbage

The cabbage can be cooked the day before and reheated for serving. It is a good accompaniment to goose, pork or strong-flavoured game dishes. The crispy bacon added at the end of cooking is optional and can be omitted.

Serves 8

INGREDIENTS

900 g/2 lb red cabbage
30 ml/2 tbsp olive oil
2 large onions, sliced
2 large cooking apples, peeled, cored
  and sliced
30 ml/2 tbsp cider vinegar
30 ml/2 tbsp soft brown sugar
225 g/8 oz rindless streaky bacon
  (optional)
salt and freshly ground black pepper

apples

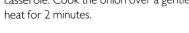

olive oil

cider vinegar

cabbage

brown sugar

streaky bacon

onions

1 Preheat the oven to 180°C/350°F/ Gas 4. Cut the cabbage into quarters through the stalk and shred it finely with a sharp knife or in a food processor, discarding the hard core.

2 Heat the oil in a large ovenproof casserole. Cook the onion over a gentle heat for 2 minutes.

3 Stir the cabbage, apples, vinegar, sugar and seasoning into the casserole. Cover with a tight-fitting lid and cook for about 1 hour, or until very tender. Stir half-way through cooking.

4 Chop the bacon, if using, and fry it gently in a pan until crisp. Stir it into the cabbage just before serving.

Vegetarian Christmas Pie

A sophisticated mushroom flan with a cheese-soufflé topping. Serve hot with cranberry relish and Brussels Sprouts with Chestnuts and Carrots.

Serves 8

INGREDIENTS
225 g/8 oz/2 cups plain flour
175 g/6 oz/¾ cup butter
10 ml/2 tsp paprika
115 g/4 oz Parmesan cheese, grated
1 egg, beaten with 15 ml/1 tbsp cold
   water
15 ml/1 tbsp Dijon mustard

FOR THE FILLING
25 g/1 oz/2 tbsp butter
1 onion, finely chopped
1–2 garlic cloves, crushed
350 g/12 oz mushrooms, chopped
10 ml/2 tsp dried mixed herbs
15 ml/1 tbsp chopped fresh parsley
50 g/2 oz/1 cup fresh white
   breadcrumbs
salt and freshly ground black pepper

FOR THE CHEESE TOPPING
25 g/1 oz/2 tbsp butter
25 g/1 oz/2 tbsp plain flour
300 ml/½ pint/1¼ cups milk
25 g/1 oz Parmesan cheese, grated
75 g/3 oz Cheddar cheese, grated
¼ tsp English mustard powder
1 egg, separated

1 To make the pastry, sift the flour into a bowl and rub in the butter until the mixture resembles fine breadcrumbs. Stir in the paprika and Parmesan cheese. Bind to a soft pliable dough with the egg and water. Knead until smooth, wrap in clear film and chill for 30 minutes.

4 For the cheese topping, melt the butter in a pan, stir in the flour and cook for 2 minutes. Gradually blend in the milk. Bring to the boil to thicken and simmer for 2–3 minutes. Remove the pan from the heat and stir in the cheeses, mustard powder and egg yolk, and season well. Beat until smooth. Whisk the egg white until it holds soft peaks; fold the egg white into the topping.

2 For the filling, melt the butter and cook the onion until tender. Add the garlic and mushrooms and cook, uncovered, for 5 minutes, stirring occasionally. Increase the heat and drive off any liquid in the pan. Remove the pan from the heat and stir in the dried herbs, parsley, breadcrumbs and seasoning. Allow to cool.

3 Preheat the oven to 190°C/375°F/ Gas 5. Put a baking tray in the oven. On a lightly floured surface, roll out the pastry and use it to line a 23 cm/9 in loose-based flan tin, pressing the pastry well into the edges and making a narrow rim around the top edge. Chill for 20 minutes.

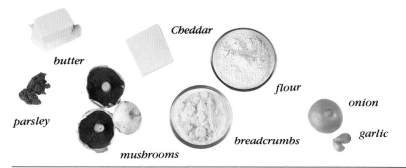

butter

Cheddar

flour

parsley

mushrooms

breadcrumbs

onion

garlic

5 To assemble the pie, spread the Dijon mustard evenly over the base of the flan case. Spoon in the mushroom filling and level the surface.

6 Pour over the cheese topping and bake the pie on the hot baking tray for 35–45 minutes until set and golden.

Game Terrine

Any game can be used to make this country terrine.
The ovenproof dish that it is cooked in must have a lid,
to seal in all the flavours during the long cooking time.

Serves 8

INGREDIENTS

225 g/8 oz rindless, unsmoked streaky
    bacon
225 g/8 oz lamb's or pig's liver,
    minced
450 g/1 lb minced pork
1 small onion, finely chopped
2 garlic cloves, crushed
10 ml/2 tsp dried mixed herbs
225 g/8 oz game (e.g., hare, rabbit,
    pheasant or pigeon)
60 ml/4 tbsp port or sherry
1 bay leaf
50 g/2 oz/4 tbsp plain flour
300 ml/½ pint/1¼ cups aspic jelly,
    made up as packet instructions
salt and freshly ground black pepper

bacon

port

herbs

pork

liver

bay leaf

onion

1 Remove the rind from the bacon and stretch each rasher with the back of a heavy knife. Use to line a 1 litre/1¾ pint/4 cup terrine.

2 In a bowl, mix together the minced meats with the onion, garlic and dried herbs. Season with salt and pepper.

3 Cut the game into thin strips and put it into a bowl with the port or sherry. Season with salt and pepper.

4 Put one-third of the minced mixture into the terrine, pressing it well into the corners. Cover with half the strips of game and repeat these layers, ending with a minced layer. Level the surface and lay the bay leaf on top.

5 Preheat the oven to 170°C/325°F/Gas 3. Put the flour into a small bowl and mix it to a firm dough with 30–45 ml/2–3 tbsp cold water. Cover the terrine with a lid and seal it with the flour paste. Place the terrine in a roasting tin and pour around enough hot water to come half-way up the sides of the dish. Cook in the oven for 2 hours.

6 Remove the lid and weight the terrine down with a 2 kg/4 lb weight. Leave to cool. Remove any fat from the Surface and cover with warmed aspic jelly. Leave overnight before turning out.

Turkey and Cranberry Pie

The cranberries add a tart layer to this turkey pie. Cranberry sauce can be used if fresh cranberries are not available. The pie freezes well.

Serves 8

INGREDIENTS
450 g/1 lb pork sausagemeat
450 g/1 lb lean minced pork
15 ml/1 tbsp ground coriander
15 ml/1 tbsp dried mixed herbs
finely grated rind of 2 large oranges
10 ml/2 tsp grated fresh root ginger or
    2.5 ml/½ tsp ground ginger
10 ml/2 tsp salt
450 g/1 lb turkey breast fillets, thinly
    sliced
115 g/4 oz fresh cranberries
freshly ground black pepper

FOR THE PASTRY
450 g/1 lb/4 cups plain flour
5 ml/1 tsp salt
150 g/5 oz/⅔ cup lard
150 ml/¼ pint/⅔ cup mixed milk and
    water

TO FINISH
1 egg, beaten
300 ml/½ pint/1¼ cups aspic jelly,
    made up as packet instructions

cranberries

turkey fillets

pork

ginger

herbs

orange

coriander

1 Preheat the oven to 180°C/350°F/ Gas 4. Place a baking tray in the oven to preheat. In a bowl, mix together the sausagemeat, pork, coriander, herbs, orange rind, ginger and salt and pepper.

2 To make the pastry, put the flour into a large bowl with the salt. Heat the lard in a small pan with the milk and water until just beginning to boil. Draw the pan aside and allow to cool slightly.

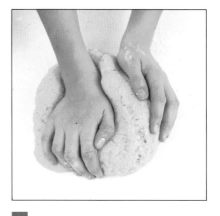

3 Using a wooden spoon, quickly stir the liquid into the flour until a very stiff dough is formed. Turn on to a work surface and knead until smooth. Cut one-third off the dough for the lid, wrap it in clear film and keep it in a warm place.

4 Roll out the large piece of dough on a floured surface and line the base and sides of a well-greased 20 cm/8 in loose-based, springform cake tin. Work with the dough while it is still warm, as it will crack and break if it is left to get cold.

5 Put the turkey breast fillets between two pieces of cling film and flatten with a rolling pin to a 3 mm/⅛ in thickness. Spoon half the pork mixture into the base of the tin, pressing it well into the edges. Cover with half of the turkey slices and then the cranberries, followed by the remaining turkey and finally the rest of the pork mixture.

6 Roll out the rest of the dough and cover the filling, trimming any excess and sealing the edges with a little beaten egg. Make a steam hole in the centre of the lid and decorate the top by cutting pastry trimmings into leaf shapes. Brush with beaten egg. Bake for 2 hours. Cover the pie with foil if the top gets too brown. Place the pie on a wire rack to cool. When cold, use a funnel to fill the pie with liquid aspic jelly. Leave to set for a few hours or overnight, before unmoulding the pie to serve it.

Turkey Rice Salad

A delicious, crunchy salad to use up leftover turkey during the holiday festivities.

Serves 8

INGREDIENTS
225 g/8 oz/1¼ cups brown rice
50 g/2 oz/⅔ cup wild rice
2 red dessert apples, quartered, cored and chopped
2 celery sticks, coarsely sliced
115 g/4 oz seedless grapes
45 ml/3 tbsp lemon or orange juice
150 ml/¼ pint/⅔ cup thick mayonnaise
350 g/12 oz cooked turkey, chopped
salt and freshly ground black pepper
frilly lettuce leaves, to serve

lettuce leaves

celery

mayonnaise

turkey

brown rice

grapes

wild rice

apples

1 Cook the brown and wild rice together in plenty of boiling salted water for 25 minutes, or until tender. Rinse under cold running water and drain thoroughly.

2 Turn into a large bowl and add the apples, celery and grapes. Beat the lemon or orange juice into the mayonnaise, season with salt and pepper and pour over the rice.

3 Add the turkey and mix well to coat with the lemon or orange mayonnaise.

4 Arrange the frilly lettuce over the base and around the sides of a serving dish and spoon the rice on top.

Ham and Bulgur Wheat Salad

This unusual, nutty salad uses up leftover cooked ham for a quick meal on Boxing Day.

Serves 8

INGREDIENTS
225 g/8 oz bulgur wheat
45 ml/3 tbsp olive oil
30 ml/2 tbsp lemon juice
1 red pepper
225 g/8 oz cooked ham, diced
30 ml/2 tbsp chopped fresh mint
30 ml/2 tbsp currants
salt and freshly ground black pepper
sprigs of fresh mint and lemon slices,
    to garnish

olive oil

mint

bulgur wheat

ham

currants

red pepper

lemon

1 Put the bulgur wheat into a bowl, pour over enough boiling water to cover and leave to stand until all the water has been absorbed.

2 Add the oil, lemon juice, and seasoning to taste. Toss to separate the grains using two forks.

3 Quarter the pepper, removing the stalk and seeds. Cut it into wide strips and then into diamonds. Add the pepper, ham, mint and currants. Transfer to a serving dish and garnish with sprigs of fresh mint and lemon slices.

COOK'S TIP

This salad can also be made with 225 g/8 oz couscous instead of the bulgur wheat. Cover the couscous with boiling water as in step 1.

Layered Salmon Terrine

This elegant fish mousse is perfect for a buffet table or first course. Slice with a sharp knife.

Serves 8

INGREDIENTS
200 ml/7 fl oz/⅞ cup milk
50 g/2 oz/4 tbsp butter
65 g/2½ oz/⅔ cup plain flour
450 g/1 lb fresh haddock fillet, boned
    and skinned
450 g/1 lb fresh salmon fillet, boned
    and skinned
2 eggs, beaten
60 ml/4 tbsp double cream
115 g/4 oz smoked salmon or trout,
    cut in strips
salt and freshly ground black pepper

1 Heat the milk and butter in a saucepan until the milk is boiling, draw the pan aside and beat in the flour until a thick smooth paste forms. Season with salt and pepper, turn out on to a plate and leave to cool.

2 Put the haddock into a food processor and process it until smooth. Put it into a bowl. Process the salmon fillet in the same way and put it into a separate bowl. Add an egg and half the cream to each of the fish mixtures. Beat in half the milk and flour paste to each mixture.

3 Preheat the oven to 180°C/350°F/Gas 4. Butter a 900 g/2 lb loaf tin and line it with a piece of greaseproof paper. Lay strips of smoked salmon or trout diagonally over the base and up the sides of the lined tin.

haddock

cream

flour

fresh salmon

butter

milk

eggs

smoked salmon

4 Carefully spoon the haddock mixture into the tin and level the surface. Cover with the salmon mixture and fold any overlapping smoked salmon strips over the filling.

5 Cover the loaf tin with a piece of buttered greaseproof paper and then a layer of foil. Place it in a roasting tin and pour round enough hot water to come halfway up the sides of the tin. Cook for 40 minutes, or until firm to the touch.

6 Remove from the oven and stand for 10 minutes. Turn the terrine out on to a serving plate and serve it warm or leave it to cool.

Fillet of Beef with Ratatouille

This succulent rare beef is served cold with a colourful garlicky ratatouille.

Serves 8

INGREDIENTS
700–900 g/1½–2 lb fillet of beef
45 ml/3 tbsp olive oil
300 ml/½ pint/1¼ cups aspic jelly,
    made up as packet instructions

FOR THE MARINADE
30 ml/2 tbsp sherry
30 ml/2 tbsp olive oil
30 ml/2 tbsp soy sauce
10 ml/2 tsp grated fresh root ginger or
    5 ml/1 tsp ground ginger
2 garlic cloves, crushed

FOR THE RATATOUILLE
60 ml/4 tbsp olive oil
1 onion, sliced
2–3 garlic cloves, crushed
1 large aubergine, cubed
1 small red pepper, seeded
    and sliced
1 small green pepper, seeded and
    sliced
1 small yellow pepper, seeded
    and sliced
225 g/8 oz courgettes, sliced
450 g/1 lb tomatoes, skinned and
    quartered
15 ml/1 tbsp chopped fresh
    mixed herbs
30 ml/2 tbsp French dressing
salt and freshly ground black pepper

aubergine

tomatoes

peppers

beef

olive oil

ginger

soy sauce

courgette

sherry

onion

1 Mix all the marinade ingredients together in a shallow dish, put the beef in and turn it over to coat it. Cover with clear film and leave for 30 minutes, to allow the flavours to penetrate the meat.

2 Preheat the oven to 220°C/425°F/ Gas 7. Lift the fillet out of the marinade and pat it dry with kitchen paper. Heat the oil in a frying-pan until smoking hot and then brown the beef all over to seal it. Transfer to a roasting tin and roast for 10–15 minutes, basting it with the marinade. Lift the beef on to a plate and leave it to cool.

3 Meanwhile, for the ratatouille, heat the oil in a large casserole and cook the onion and garlic over a low heat until tender. Add the aubergine and cook for a further 5 minutes, until soft. Add the sliced peppers and courgettes and cook for 2 minutes. Then add the tomatoes, herbs and seasoning and cook for a few minutes longer.

4 Turn the ratatouille into a dish and cool. Drizzle with a little French dressing. Slice the beef and arrange overlapping slices on a serving platter. Brush the slices with cold, aspic jelly which is on the point of setting.

5 Leave the jelly to set completely, then brush with a second coat. Spoon the ratatouille on to the dish and serve.

Salmon and Pea Ring

A stunning pea and fish mousse with salmon chunks set in it. Serve it hot or cold as a starter, with a delicious herb and lemon sauce.

Serves 8

INGREDIENTS
450 g/1 lb fresh haddock, filleted, skinned and cubed
115 g/4 oz frozen peas, cooked and cooled
2 eggs
60 ml/4 tbsp double cream
450 g/1 lb fresh salmon, filleted, skinned and cubed
salt and freshly ground black pepper
small bunch watercress, to garnish

FOR THE HERB AND LEMON SAUCE
150 ml/¼ pint/⅔ cup fish stock
225 g/8 oz low-fat cream cheese
15 ml/1 tbsp lemon juice
15 ml/1 tbsp chopped fresh parsley
15 ml/1 tbsp snipped fresh chives

1 Check the fish for any stray bones. Preheat the oven to 180°C/350°F/Gas 4. Put the haddock and cooked peas into a food processor and process them until smooth.

2 Add the eggs, cream and seasoning to the food processor and mix together thoroughly.

3 Transfer to a bowl and fold in the cubed salmon pieces. Butter a 1 litre/1¾ pint/4 cup ring mould and spoon in the fish mixture. Level the top and cover it with buttered paper and foil. Put the ring mould into a roasting tin and pour round hot water to come half-way up the sides of the tin. Poach in the oven for 40 minutes, or until firm to the touch.

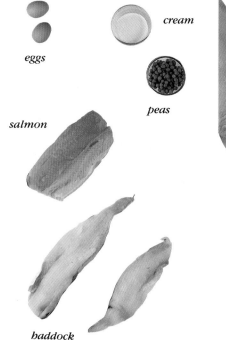

cream

eggs

peas

salmon

haddock

4 Meanwhile, make the sauce. Put the fish stock and cream cheese in a pan and heat gently to melt. Whisk until smooth. Add the lemon juice and herbs and season to taste. Turn the fish mould out on to a serving plate and garnish it with a bunch of watercress in the centre. Serve it warm or cold, with the sauce.

Chocolate and Chestnut Yule Log

This is based on the French Bûche de Noël, traditionally served at Christmas. Make it the day before or some time in advance and freeze it. It's an excellent dessert for a party.

Serves 8

INGREDIENTS
25 g/1 oz/2 tbsp plain flour
30 ml/2 tbsp cocoa powder
pinch of salt
3 large eggs, separated
large pinch of cream of tartar
115 g/4 oz/8 tbsp caster sugar
2–3 drops almond essence
sifted cocoa powder and holly sprigs,
   to decorate

FOR THE FILLING
15 ml/1 tbsp rum or brandy
5 ml/1 tsp powdered gelatine
115 g/4 oz dark chocolate, broken
   into squares
50 g/2 oz/4 tbsp caster sugar
250 g/8 oz canned chestnut purée
300 ml/½ pint/1¼ cups double cream

chestnut purée   *flour*

cream of tartar

cocoa powder

brandy   *cream*

dark chocolate   *eggs*   *almond essence*

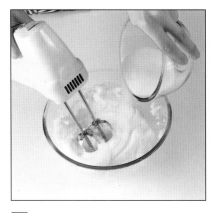

1 Preheat the oven to 180°C/350°F/ Gas 4. Grease and line a 23 × 33 cm/9 × 13 in Swiss roll tin and line the base with non-stick silicone paper. Sift the flour, cocoa and salt together on to a piece of greaseproof paper.

2 Put the egg whites into a large clean bowl and whisk them until frothy. Add the cream of tartar and whisk until stiff. Gradually whisk in half the sugar, until the mixture will stand in stiff peaks.

3 Put the egg yolks and the remaining sugar into another bowl and whisk until thick and pale. Add the almond essence. Stir in the sifted flour and cocoa mixture. Lastly, fold in the egg whites, using a metal spoon, until everything is evenly blended. Be careful not to over mix.

4 Turn the mixture into the prepared Swiss roll tin and level the top. Bake for 15–20 minutes, or until springy to the touch. Have ready a large piece of greaseproof paper dusted liberally with caster sugar. Turn the Swiss roll on to the paper, remove the silicone lining paper, and roll it up with the greaseproof paper still inside. Leave to cool completely on a wire rack.

5 Put the brandy in a cup and sprinkle over the gelatine; leave to become spongy. Melt the chocolate in a 600 ml/ 1 pint/2½ cup basin over a pan of hot water. Melt the gelatine over hot water and add to the chocolate. With an electric beater, whisk in the sugar and chestnut purée. Remove from the heat and leave to cool. Whisk the cream until it holds soft peaks. Fold the two mixtures together evenly.

6 Unroll the cake carefully, spread it with half the filling and roll it up again. Place it on a serving dish and spread over the rest of the chocolate cream to cover it. Mark it with a fork to resemble a log. Chill until firm. Dust the cake with sifted cocoa powder and decorate the plate with sprigs of holly.

Ginger Trifle

This is a good way to use up leftover cake, whether plain, chocolate or gingerbread. You can substitute runny honey for the ginger and syrup, if you prefer. This pudding can be made the day before.

Serves 8

INGREDIENTS
225 g/8 oz gingerbread or other cake
60 ml/4 tbsp Grand Marnier or
   sweet sherry
2 ripe dessert pears, peeled, cored
   and cubed
2 bananas, thickly sliced
2 oranges, segmented
1–2 pieces stem ginger, finely
   chopped, plus 30 ml/2 tbsp syrup

FOR THE CUSTARD
2 eggs
50 g/2 oz/4 tbsp caster sugar
15 ml/1 tbsp cornflour
450 ml/¾ pint/1⅞ cups milk
few drops vanilla essence

TO DECORATE
150 ml/¼ pint/⅔ cup double cream,
   lightly whipped
25 g/1 oz/¼ cup chopped almonds,
   toasted
4 glacé cherries
8 small pieces angelica

gingerbread
bananas
pear
orange
eggs
glacé cherries

1 Cut the gingerbread into 4 cm/1½ in cubes. Put them in the bottom of a 1.75 litre/3 pint/7½ cup glass bowl. Sprinkle over the Grand Marnier or sherry and leave to soak in.

2 To make the custard, whisk the eggs, sugar and cornflour together in a bowl with a little of the milk. Heat the remaining milk until it is almost boiling. Pour it on to the egg mixture, whisking all the time. Return to the pan and stir over the heat until thickened. Simmer for 2 minutes, to cook the cornflour. Add the vanilla essence and leave to cool.

3 Mix all the prepared fruit with the finely chopped stem ginger and syrup. Spoon into the bowl on top of the gingerbread. Spoon over the custard to cover and chill until set.

4 Cover the top with whipped cream and scatter on the toasted almonds. Arrange the glacé cherries and angelica around the edge.

Ruby Fruit Salad

After a rich main course, this port-flavoured fruit salad is light and refreshing. Use any fruit that is available.

Serves 8

INGREDIENTS

300 ml/½ pint/1¼ cups water
115 g/4 oz/8 tbsp caster sugar
1 cinnamon stick
4 cloves
pared rind of 1 orange
300 ml/½ pint/1¼ cups port
2 oranges
1 small ripe Ogen, Charentais or honeydew melon
4 small bananas
2 dessert apples
225 g/8 oz seedless grapes

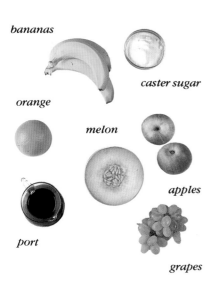

bananas

caster sugar

orange

melon

apples

port

grapes

1 Put the water, sugar, spices and pared orange rind into a pan and stir over a gentle heat to dissolve the sugar. Then bring to the boil, cover with a lid and simmer for 10 minutes. Leave to cool, then add the port.

2 Strain the liquid (to remove the spices and orange rind) into a bowl. With a sharp knife, cut off all the skin and pith from the oranges. Then, holding each orange over the bowl to catch the juice, cut away the segments, by slicing between the membrane that divides each segment and allowing the segments to drop into the syrup. Squeeze the remaining pith to release any juice.

3 Cut the melon in half, remove the seeds and scoop out the flesh with a melon baller, or cut it in small cubes. Add it to the syrup.

4 Peel the bananas and cut them diagonally in 1 cm/½ in slices. Quarter and core the apples and cut them in small cubes. Leave the skin on, or peel them if it is tough. Halve the grapes if large or leave them whole. Stir all the fruit into the syrup, cover with clear film and chill for an hour before serving.

Christmas Pudding

This recipe makes enough to fill one 1.2 litre/2 pint/ 5 cup basin or two 600 ml/1 pint/2½ cup basins. It can be made up to a month before Christmas and stored in a cool, dry place. Steam the pudding for 2 hours before serving. Serve with brandy or rum butter, whisky sauce, custard or whipped cream, topped with a decorative sprig of holly.

Serves 8

INGREDIENTS
115 g/4 oz/½ cup butter
225 g/8 oz/1 heaped cup soft dark brown sugar
50 g/2 oz/½ cup self-raising flour
5 ml/1 tsp ground mixed spice
¼ tsp grated nutmeg
2.5 ml/½ tsp ground cinnamon
2 eggs
115 g/4 oz/2 cups fresh white breadcrumbs
175 g/6 oz/1 cup sultanas
175 g/6 oz/1 cup raisins
115 g/4 oz/½ cup currants
25 g/1 oz/3 tbsp mixed candied peel, chopped finely
25 g/1 oz/¼ cup chopped almonds
1 small cooking apple, peeled, cored and coarsely grated
finely grated rind of 1 orange or lemon
juice of 1 orange or lemon, made up to 150 ml/¼ pint/⅔ cup with brandy, rum or sherry

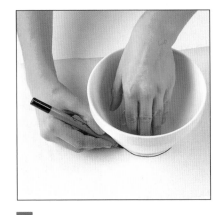

peel

nutmeg

cinnamon

almonds

breadcrumbs

raisins

sultanas

currants

brown sugar

orange

butter

apple

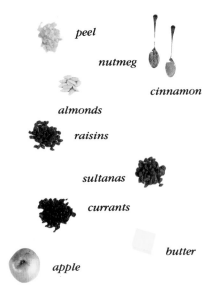

1 Cut a disc of greaseproof paper to fit the base of the basin(s) and butter the disc and basin(s).

2 Whisk the butter and sugar together until soft. Beat in the flour, spices and eggs. Stir in the remaining ingredients thoroughly. The mixture should have a soft dropping consistency.

3 Turn the mixture into the greased basin(s) and level the top.

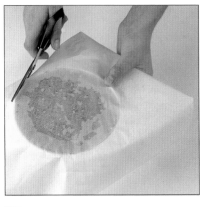

4 Cover with another disc of buttered greaseproof paper.

5 Make a pleat across the centre of a large piece of greaseproof paper and cover the basin(s) with it, tying it in place with string under the rim. Cut off the excess paper. Pleat a piece of foil in the same way and cover the basin(s) with it, tucking it around the bowl neatly, under the greaseproof frill. Tie another piece of string around the basin(s) and across the top, as a handle.

6 Place the basin(s) in a steamer over a pan of simmering water and steam for 6 hours. Alternatively, put the basin(s) into a large pan and pour round enough boiling water to come halfway up the basin(s) and cover the pan with a tight-fitting lid. Check the water is simmering and top it up with boiling water as it evaporates. When the pudding(s) have cooked, leave to cool completely. Then remove the foil and greaseproof paper. Wipe the basin(s) clean and replace the greaseproof paper and foil with clean pieces, ready for reheating.

TO SERVE

Steam for 2 hours. Turn on to a plate and leave to stand for 5 minutes, before removing the pudding basin (the steam will rise to the top of the basin and help to loosen the pudding).

De Luxe Mincemeat Tart

The mincemeat can be made up and kept in the fridge for up to two weeks. It can also be used to make individual mince pies.

Serves 8

INGREDIENTS

225 g/8 oz/2 cups plain flour
10 ml/2 tsp ground cinnamon
50 g/2 oz/⅔ cup walnuts, finely ground
115 g/4 oz/½ cup butter
50 g/2 oz/4 tbsp caster sugar, plus
    extra for dusting
1 egg
2 drops vanilla essence
15 ml/1 tbsp cold water

FOR THE MINCEMEAT

2 dessert apples, peeled, cored and
    coarsely grated
225 g/8 oz/1⅓ cups raisins
115 g/4 oz no-soak dried apricots,
    chopped
115 g/4 oz no-soak dried figs or
    prunes, chopped
225 g/8 oz green grapes, halved and
    seeded
50 g/2 oz/½ cup chopped almonds
finely grated rind of 1 lemon
30 ml/2 tbsp lemon juice
30 ml/2 tbsp brandy or port
¼ tsp ground mixed spice
115 g/4 oz/generous ½ cup soft light
    brown sugar
25 g/1 oz/2 tbsp butter, melted

1 To make the pastry, put the flour, cinnamon and walnuts in a food processor. Add the butter and process until the mixture resembles fine breadcrumbs. Turn into a bowl and stir in the sugar. Using a fork, beat the egg with the vanilla essence and water. Gradually stir the egg mixture into the dry ingredients. Gather together with your fingertips to form a soft, pliable dough. Knead briefly on a lightly floured surface until smooth; then wrap the dough in clear film and chill it for 30 minutes.

2 Mix all the mincemeat ingredients together thoroughly in a bowl.

3 Cut one-third off the pastry and reserve it for the lattice. Roll out the remainder and use it to line a 23 cm/9 in, loose-based flan tin. Take care to push the pastry well into the edges and make a 5 mm/¼ in rim around the top edge.

4 With a rolling pin, roll off the excess pastry to neaten the edge. Fill the pastry case with the mincemeat.

brandy
raisins
almonds
grapes
brown sugar
walnuts
flour
lemon
apple
butter
apricots
figs

5 Roll out the remaining pastry and cut it into 1 cm/½ in strips. Arrange the strips in a lattice over the top of the pastry, wet the joins and press them together well. Chill for 30 minutes.

6 Preheat the oven to 190°C/375°F/ Gas 5. Place a baking sheet in the oven to preheat. Brush the pastry with water and dust it with caster sugar. Bake it on the baking sheet for 30–40 minutes. Transfer to a wire rack and leave to cool for 15 minutes. Then carefully remove the flan tin. Serve warm or cold, with sweetened, whipped cream.

Iced Praline Torte

Make this elaborate torte several days ahead, decorate it and return it to the freezer until you are nearly ready to serve it. Allow the torte to stand at room temperature for an hour before serving, or leave it in the refrigerator overnight to soften.

Serves 8

INGREDIENTS

115 g/4 oz/1 cup almonds or
   hazelnuts
115 g/4 oz/8 tbsp caster sugar
115 g/4 oz/⅔ cup raisins
90 ml/6 tbsp rum or brandy
115 g/4 oz dark chocolate, broken
   into squares
30 ml/2 tbsp milk
450 ml/¾ pint/1⅞ cups double cream
30 ml/2 tbsp strong black coffee
16 sponge-finger biscuits

TO FINISH

150 ml/¼ pint/⅔ cup double cream
50 g/2 oz/½ cup almonds, toasted
15 g/½ oz dark chocolate, melted

biscuits

double cream

dark chocolate

black coffee

almonds

raisins

brandy

1 To make the praline, have ready an oiled cake tin or baking sheet. Put the nuts into a heavy-based pan with the sugar and heat gently until the sugar melts. Swirl the pan to coat the nuts in the hot sugar. Cook slowly until the nuts brown and the sugar caramelizes. Watch all the time, as this will only take a few minutes. Turn the nuts quickly into the tin or on to the tray and leave them to cool completely. Break them up and grind them to a fine powder in a food processor.

2 Soak the raisins in 45 ml/3 tbsp of the rum or brandy for an hour (or better still overnight), so they soften and absorb the rum. Melt the chocolate with the milk in a bowl over a pan of hot, but not boiling water. Remove and allow to cool. Lightly grease a 1.2 litre/2 pint/5 cup loaf tin and line it with greaseproof paper.

3 Whisk the cream in a bowl until it holds soft peaks. Whisk in the cold chocolate. Then fold in the praline and the soaked raisins, with any liquid.

4 Mix the coffee and remaining rum or brandy in a shallow dish. Dip in the sponge-fingers and arrange half in a layer over the base of the prepared loaf tin.

5 Cover with the chocolate mixture and add another layer of soaked sponge-fingers. Freeze overnight.

6 Dip the tin briefly into warm water to loosen it and turn the torte out on to a serving plate. Cover with whipped cream. Sprinkle the top with toasted flaked almonds and drizzle the melted chocolate over the top. Return the torte to the freezer until it's needed.

Spiced Pears in Red Wine

Serve these pears hot or cold, with lightly whipped cream. The flavours improve with keeping, so you can make this several days before you want it.

Serves 8

INGREDIENTS
600 ml/1 pint/2½ cups red wine
225 g/8 oz/1⅛ cups caster sugar
cinnamon stick
6 cloves
finely grated rind of 1 orange
10 ml/2 tsp grated root ginger
8 even-sized firm pears, with stalks
15 ml/1 tbsp brandy
25 g/1 oz/ 2 tbsp almonds or hazelnuts, toasted, to decorate

red wine

caster sugar

pears

orange

brandy

almonds

cinnamon sticks

1 Choose a pan large enough to hold all the pears upright in one layer. Put all the ingredients except the pears, brandy and almonds into the pan and heat slowly until the sugar has dissolved. Simmer for 5 minutes.

2 Peel the pears, leaving the stalks on, and cut away the flower end. Arrange them upright in the pan. Cover with a lid and simmer *very* gently until they are tender. The cooking time will vary depending on their size and how ripe they are, but will be about 45–50 minutes.

3 Remove the pears from the syrup with a slotted spoon, being careful not to pull out the stalks. Put them in a serving bowl or individual bowls.

4 Bring the syrup to the boil and boil it rapidly until it thickens and reduces. Allow to cool slightly, add the brandy and strain over the pears. Scatter on the toasted nuts to decorate.

Frozen Grand Marnier Soufflés

These sophisticated little puddings are always appreciated and make a wonderful end to a meal.

Serves 8

INGREDIENTS
200 g/7 oz/1 cup caster sugar
6 large eggs, separated
250 ml/8 fl oz/1 cup milk
15 g/½ oz powdered gelatine, soaked
    in 45 ml/3 tbsp cold water
450 ml/¾ pint/1⅞ cups double cream
60 ml/4 tbsp Grand Marnier

cream

Grand Marnier

eggs

caster sugar

gelatine

1 Tie a double-collar of greaseproof paper around eight ramekin dishes. Put 75 g/3 oz/6 tbsp of the sugar in a bowl with the egg yolks and whisk until pale.

2 Heat the milk until almost boiling and pour it on to the yolks, whisking all the time. Return to the pan and stir it over a gentle heat until it is thick enough to coat the spoon. Remove the pan from the heat. Stir the soaked gelatine into the custard. Pour into a bowl and leave to cool. Whisk occasionally, until the custard is on the point of setting.

3 Put the remaining sugar in a pan with the water and dissolve it over a low heat. Bring to the boil and boil rapidly until it reaches the soft ball stage or 118°C/240°F on a sugar thermometer. Remove from the heat. In a clean bowl, whisk the egg whites until they are stiff. Pour the hot syrup on to the whites, whisking all the time. Leave to cool.

4 Whisk the cream until it holds soft peaks. Add the Grand Marnier to the cold custard and fold the custard into the cold meringue, with the cream. Quickly pour into the prepared ramekin dishes. Freeze overnight. Remove the paper collars. Leave the soufflés at room temperature for 30 minutes before serving.

White Amaretto Mousses with Chocolate Sauce

These little desserts are extremely rich, and derive their flavour from Amaretto, an almond-flavoured liqueur, and amaretti, little almond-flavoured biscuits.

Serves 8

INGREDIENTS
115 g/4 oz amaretti, ratafia or
  macaroon biscuits
60 ml/4 tbsp Amaretto liqueur
350 g/12 oz white chocolate, broken
  into squares
15 g/½ oz powdered gelatine, soaked
  in 45 ml/3 tbsp cold water
450 ml/¾ pint/1⅞ cups double cream

FOR THE CHOCOLATE SAUCE
225 g/8 oz dark chocolate, broken
  into squares
300 ml/½ pint/1¼ cups single cream
50 g/2 oz/4 tbsp caster sugar

cream

amaretti biscuits

Amaretto

white chocolate

dark chocolate

caster sugar

1 Lightly oil eight individual 120 ml/ 4 fl oz moulds and line the base of each mould with a small disc of oiled greaseproof paper. Put the biscuits into a large bowl and crush them finely with a rolling pin.

2 Melt the Amaretto and white chocolate together gently in a bowl over a pan of hot but not boiling water (be very careful not to overheat the chocolate). Stir well until smooth; remove from the pan and leave to cool.

3 Melt the gelatine over hot water and blend it into the chocolate mixture. Whisk the cream until it holds soft peaks. Fold in the chocolate mixture, with 60 ml/4 tbsp of the crushed biscuits.

4 Put a teaspoonful of the crushed biscuits into the bottom of each mould and spoon in the chocolate mixture. Tap each mould to disperse any air bubbles. Level the tops and sprinkle the remaining crushed biscuits on top. Press down gently and chill for 4 hours.

5 To make the chocolate sauce, put all the ingredients in a small pan and heat gently to melt the chocolate and dissolve the sugar. Simmer for 2–3 minutes. Leave to cool completely.

6 Slip a knife around the sides of each mould, and turn out on to individual plates. Remove the greaseproof paper and pour round a little dark chocolate sauce.

Crunchy Apple and Almond Flan

Do not be tempted to put any sugar with the apples, as this makes them produce too much liquid. All the sweetness is in the pastry and topping.

Serves 8

INGREDIENTS
75 g/3 oz/6 tbsp butter
175 g/6 oz/1½ cups plain flour
25 g/1 oz/scant ⅓ cup ground almonds
25 g/1 oz/2 tbsp caster sugar
1 egg yolk
15 ml/1 tbsp cold water
¼ tsp almond essence
sifted icing sugar, to decorate

FOR THE CRUNCHY TOPPING
115 g/4 oz/1 cup plain flour
¼ tsp ground mixed spice
50 g/2 oz/4 tbsp butter, cut in small cubes
50 g/2 oz/4 tbsp demerara sugar
50 g/2 oz/½ cup flaked almonds

FOR THE FILLING
675 g/1½ lb cooking apples
25 g/1 oz/2 tbsp raisins or sultanas

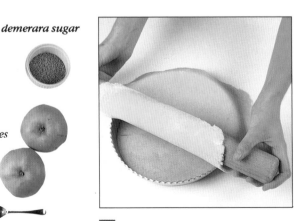

demerara sugar
flour
raisins
apples
butter
almond essence

1 To make the pastry, rub the butter, by hand or in a processor, into the flour until it resembles fine breadcrumbs. Stir in the ground almonds and sugar. Whisk the egg yolk, water and almond essence together and mix them into the dry ingredients to form a soft, pliable dough. Knead the dough lightly until smooth, wrap in clear film and leave in a cool place to rest for 20 minutes.

4 Roll off the excess pastry to neaten the edge. Chill for 15 minutes.

2 Meanwhile, make the crunchy topping. Sift the flour and mixed spice into a bowl and rub in the butter. Stir in the sugar and almonds.

5 Preheat the oven to 190°C/375°F/ Gas 5. Place a baking sheet in the oven to preheat. Peel, core and slice the apples thinly. Arrange the slices in the flan in overlapping, concentric circles, doming the centre. Scatter over the raisins or sultanas. The flan will seem too full at this stage, but as the apples cook the filling will drop slightly.

3 Roll out the pastry on a lightly floured surface and use it to line a 23 cm/9 in loose-based flan tin, taking care to press it neatly into the edges and to make a lip around the top edge.

6 Cover the apples with the crunchy topping mixture, pressing it on lightly. Bake on the hot baking sheet for 25–30 minutes, or until the top is golden brown and the apples are tender (test them with a fine skewer). Leave the flan to cool in the tin for 10 minutes. Serve warm or cold, dusted with sifted icing sugar.

Moist and Rich Christmas Cake

The cake can be made 4–6 weeks before Christmas. During this time, pierce the cake with a fine needle and spoon over 30–45 ml/2–3 tbsp brandy.

Makes 1 cake

INGREDIENTS
225 g/8 oz/1⅓ cups sultanas
225 g/8 oz/1 cup currants
225 g/8 oz/1⅓ cups raisins
115 g/4 oz/1 cup prunes, stoned and chopped
50 g/2 oz/¼ cup glacé cherries, halved
50 g/2 oz/⅓ cup mixed candied citrus peel, chopped
45 ml/3 tbsp brandy or sherry
225 g/8 oz/2 cups plain flour
pinch of salt
2.5 ml/½ tsp ground cinnamon
2.5 ml/½ tsp grated nutmeg
15 ml/1 tbsp cocoa powder
225 g/8 oz/1 cup butter
225 g/8 oz/1 generous cup soft dark brown sugar
4 large eggs
finely grated rind of 1 orange or lemon
50 g/2 oz/⅔ cup ground almonds
50 g/2 oz/½ cup chopped almonds

TO DECORATE
60 ml/4 tbsp apricot jam
25 cm/10 in round cake board
450 g/1 lb almond paste
450 g/1 lb white fondant icing
225 g/8 oz royal icing
1½ m/1½ yd ribbon

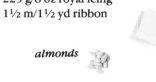

almonds

nutmeg

cinnamon

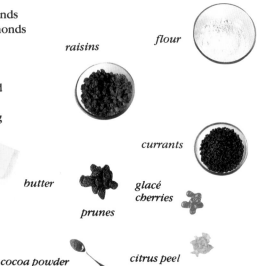

raisins

butter

prunes

glacé cherries

cocoa powder

citrus peel

flour

currants

1 The day before you want to bake the cake, put all the dried fruit to soak in the brandy or sherry, cover it with clear film and leave overnight. Grease a 20 cm/8 in round cake tin and line it with a double thickness of greaseproof paper.

2 The next day, preheat the oven to 170°C/325°F/Gas 3. Sift together the flour, salt, spices and cocoa powder. Whisk the butter and sugar together until light and fluffy and beat in the eggs gradually. Finally mix in the orange or lemon rind, the ground and chopped almonds, dried fruits (with any liquid) and the flour mixture.

4 Warm then sieve the apricot jam to make a glaze. Remove the paper from the cake and place it in the centre of the cake board and brush it with hot apricot glaze. Cover the cake with a layer of almond paste and then a layer of fondant icing. Pipe a border around the base of the cake with royal icing. Tie a ribbon around the sides.

3 Spoon into the prepared cake tin, level the top and give the cake tin a gentle tap on the work surface to settle the mixture and disperse any air bubbles. Bake for 3 hours, or until a fine skewer inserted into the middle comes out clean. Transfer the cake tin to a wire rack and let the cake cool in the tin for an hour. Then carefully turn the cake out on to the wire rack, but leave the paper on, as it will help to keep the cake moist during storage. When the cake is cold, wrap it tightly in foil and store it in a cool place.

5 Roll out any trimmings from the fondant icing and stamp out 12 small holly leaves with a cutter. Make one bell motif with a biscuit mould, dusted first with sifted icing sugar. Roll 36 small balls for the holly berries. Leave on greaseproof paper to dry for 24 hours. Decorate the cake with the leaves, berries and bell, attaching them with a little royal icing.

Nut and Glacé Fruit Ring

The cake can be made two or three weeks before Christmas. Store it in a tin in a cool place until needed.

Makes 1 ring

INGREDIENTS

115 g/4 oz/½ cup glacé cherries, quartered
115 g/4 oz/⅔ cup raisins or sultanas
115 g/4 oz dried apricots, quartered
115 g/4 oz/1 cup prunes, stoned and quartered
115 g/4 oz/½ cup stoned and chopped dates
60 ml/4 tbsp rum, brandy or sherry
115 g/4 oz/½ cup butter
115 g/4 oz/½ cup soft dark brown sugar
2.5 ml/½ tsp ground cinnamon
2.5 ml/½ tsp ground mixed spice
2 eggs, beaten
50 g/2 oz/⅔ cup ground almonds
115 g/4 oz/1 cup coarsely chopped walnuts
225 g/8 oz/2 cups self-raising flour

TO FINISH

30 ml/2 tbsp rum, brandy or sherry
60 ml/4 tbsp apricot jam
whole blanched almonds, split
3 glacé cherries, halved
few strips angelica

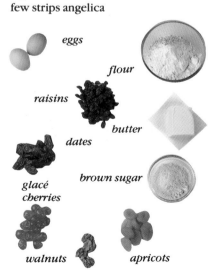

eggs

flour

raisins

butter

dates

brown sugar

glacé cherries

walnuts

apricots

1 The day before you want to bake the cake, soak all the dried fruit in the rum, brandy or sherry. Cover with clear film and leave overnight. Grease a 23 cm/9 in ring mould, with a 1.5 litre/2½ pint/6¼ cup capacity.

2 The next day, preheat the oven to 170°C/325°F/Gas 3. In a large bowl, whisk the butter, sugar and spices together until they are light and fluffy. Whisk in the eggs, and then fold in the drained, soaked fruits, with any liquid. Mix in the ground almonds, walnuts and flour.

3 Spoon the mixture into the prepared cake tin, level the top and bake for 1½–2 hours. Leave to cool in the tin for 30 minutes then turn out on to a wire rack to cool completely. Brush with the rum, brandy or sherry.

4 Put the apricot jam in a small pan and heat it gently to melt it. Sieve the jam. Brush the hot glaze over the top of the cake. Arrange the nuts and fruit in a flower design on top of the cake and brush them liberally with more apricot glaze, which must be used very hot, or the decoration will lift while you are brushing the jam over it.

Light Jewelled Fruit Cake

If you want to cover the cake with marzipan and icing omit the whole-almond decoration. The cake can be made up to two weeks before eating it. For serving, brush the top with hot apricot jam and tie a pretty ribbon around the sides.

Makes 1 cake

INGREDIENTS
115 g/4 oz/½ cup currants
115 g/4 oz/⅔ cup sultanas
225 g/8 oz/1 cup glacé cherries
 (mixed red, green and yellow),
 quartered
50 g/2 oz/½ cup mixed candied peel,
 finely chopped
30 ml/2 tbsp rum, brandy or sherry
225 g/8 oz/1 cup butter
225 g/8 oz/1⅛ cups caster sugar
finely grated rind of 1 orange
finely grated rind of 1 lemon
4 eggs
50 g/2 oz/½ cup chopped almonds
50 g/2 oz/⅔ cup ground almonds
225 g/8 oz/2 cups plain flour

TO FINISH
50 g/2 oz whole blanched almonds
 (optional)
15 ml/1 tbsp apricot jam

peel

glacé cherries

flour

sultanas

butter

orange

lemon

eggs   ground almonds

1 The day before you want to bake the cake, soak the currants, sultanas, glacé cherries and the mixed peel in the rum, brandy or sherry. Cover with clear film and leave overnight. Grease and line a 20 cm/8 in round cake tin or an 18 cm/7 in square cake tin with a double thickness of greaseproof paper.

2 The next day, preheat the oven to 170°C/325°F/Gas 3. In a large bowl, whisk the butter, sugar and orange and lemon rinds together until they are light and fluffy. Beat in the eggs, one at a time.

3 Mix in the chopped almonds, ground almonds, soaked fruits (with their liquid) and the flour, to make a soft dropping consistency. Spoon into the cake tin and level the top. Bake for 30 minutes.

4 Arrange the whole almonds in a pattern on top of the cake. Do not press them into the cake or they will sink during cooking. Return the cake to the oven and cook for a further 1½–2 hours, or until the centre is firm to the touch. Let the cake cool in the tin for 30 minutes. Then remove it and let it cool completely on a wire rack, but leave the paper on, as it helps to keep the cake moist while it is stored. When cold, wrap the cake in foil and store it in a cool place. Remove the paper before serving, and heat then sieve the apricot jam. Brush the glaze over the cake. Allow to cool.

Passion Cake

A complete change from the traditional rich Christmas cake. The icing thickens quickly as it cools and will become difficult to spread, so have the cake on a serving plate and a palette knife ready to spread the icing once it is ready. The cake will stay moist for days.

Serves 8

INGREDIENTS
150 g/5 oz/10 tbsp butter
200 g/7 oz/scant 1 cup soft light
    brown sugar
2 eggs, beaten
175 g/6 oz carrots, finely grated
finely grated rind of 1 orange
large pinch of salt
5 ml/1 tsp ground cinnamon
2.5 ml/½ tsp grated nutmeg
200 g/7 oz/1¾ cups self-raising flour
5 ml/1 tsp baking powder
115 g/4 oz/⅔ cup raisins
50 g/2 oz/½ cup chopped walnuts
30 ml/2 tbsp milk

FOR THE ICING
450 g/1 lb/2¼ cups granulated sugar
150 ml/¼ pint/⅔ cup water
pinch of cream of tartar
2 egg whites

flour

carrots

orange

butter

walnuts

brown sugar

eggs

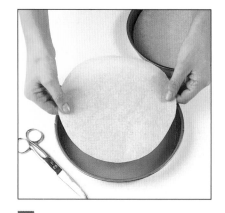

1 Preheat the oven to 190°C/375°F/Gas 5. Grease and line the bases of two 20 cm/8 in sandwich tins.

2 In a bowl, whisk together the butter and sugar until pale and fluffy. Beat in the eggs gradually, and then stir in the remaining ingredients to make a soft dropping consistency.

3 Spoon the mixture into the prepared cake tins and bake for 25–30 minutes, or until the cakes are firm to the touch. Let the cakes cool in the tins for 5 minutes. Then turn out on to a wire rack and leave to cool completely.

4 For the icing, put the sugar and water in a pan and heat them very gently to dissolve the sugar. (Swirl the pan to mix the sugar, do not stir it with a spoon.) Add the cream of tartar and bring to the boil. Boil to 115°C/240°F or to the soft ball stage. Quickly dip the base of the pan in cold water. Whisk the egg whites until they are stiff and pour the syrup over them, whisking all the time. Continue whisking until the icing loses its satiny appearance and will hold its shape. Quickly sandwich the cakes with the icing and spread the rest over the cake.

Almond Mincemeat Tartlets

These little tartlets are a welcome change from traditional mince pies. Serve them warm with brandy- or rum-flavoured custard. They freeze well and can be reheated for serving.

Makes 36

INGREDIENTS
275 g/10 oz/2½ cups plain flour
75 g/3 oz/generous ¾ cup icing sugar
5 ml/1 tsp ground cinnamon
175 g/6 oz/¾ cup butter
50 g/2 oz/⅔ cup ground almonds
1 egg yolk
45 ml/3 tbsp milk
450 g/1 lb jar mincemeat
15 ml/1 tbsp brandy or rum

FOR THE LEMON SPONGE FILLING
115 g/4 oz/½ cup butter or margarine
115 g/4 oz/8 tbsp caster sugar
175 g/6 oz/1½ cups self-raising flour
2 large eggs
finely grated rind of 1 large lemon

FOR THE LEMON ICING
115 g/4 oz/1 generous cup icing sugar
15 ml/1 tbsp lemon juice

butter

flour

brandy

eggs

icing sugar

mincemeat

ground almonds

1 For the pastry, sift the flour, icing sugar and cinnamon into a bowl or a food processor and rub in the butter until it resembles fine breadcrumbs. Add the ground almonds and bind with the egg yolk and milk to a soft, pliable dough. Knead the dough until smooth, wrap it in clear film and chill it for 30 minutes.

2 Preheat the oven to 190°C/375°F/ Gas 5. On a lightly floured surface, roll out the pastry and cut out 36 fluted rounds, to line the patty tins, with a pastry cutter. Mix the mincemeat with the brandy or rum and put a small teaspoonful in the bottom of each pastry case. Chill.

3 For the lemon sponge filling, whisk the butter or margarine, sugar, flour, eggs and lemon rind together until smooth. Spoon on top of the mincemeat, dividing it evenly, and level the tops. Bake for 20–30 minutes, or until golden brown and springy to the touch. Remove and leave to cool on a wire rack.

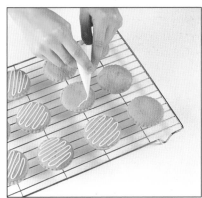

4 For the lemon icing, sift the icing sugar and mix with the lemon juice to a smooth, thick, coating consistency. Spoon into a piping bag and drizzle a zigzag pattern over each tart. If you're short of time, simply dust the tartlets with sifted icing sugar.

Christmas Biscuits

These are great fun for children to make as presents. Any shape of biscuit cutter can be used. Store them in an airtight tin. For a change, omit the lemon rind and add 25 g/1 oz/⅓ cup of ground almonds and a few drops of almond essence.

Makes about 12

INGREDIENTS
75 g/3 oz/6 tbsp butter
50 g/2 oz/generous ½ cup icing sugar
finely grated rind of 1 small lemon
1 egg yolk
175 g/6 oz/1½ cups plain flour
pinch of salt

TO DECORATE
2 egg yolks
red and green edible food colouring

1 In a large bowl, beat the butter, sugar and lemon rind together until pale and fluffy. Beat in the egg yolk, and then sift in the flour and the salt. Knead together to form a smooth dough. Wrap in clear film and chill for 30 minutes.

2 Preheat the oven to 190°C/375°F/Gas 5. On a lightly floured surface, roll out the dough to 3 mm/⅛ in thick. Using a 6 cm/2½ in fluted cutter, stamp out as many biscuits as you can, with the cutter dipped in flour to prevent it from sticking to the dough.

3 Transfer the biscuits on to lightly greased baking trays. Mark the tops lightly with a 2.5 cm/1 in holly leaf cutter and use a 5 mm/¼ in plain piping nozzle for the berries. Chill for 10 minutes, until firm.

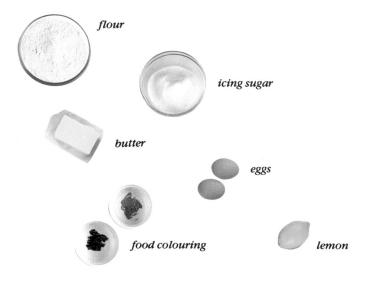

flour

icing sugar

butter

eggs

food colouring

lemon

4 Meanwhile, put each egg yolk into a small cup. Mix red food colouring into one and green food colouring into the other. Using a small, clean paintbrush, carefully paint the colours on to the biscuits. Bake the biscuits for 10–12 minutes, or until they begin to colour around the edges. Let them cool slightly on the baking trays, and then transfer them to a wire rack to cool completely.

Shortbread

You can also roll the dough out and cut it into fluted rounds, or press it into an 18 cm/7 in tin and cut it into bars.

Makes 1 × 20 cm/8 in round

INGREDIENTS
115 g/4 oz/½ cup butter
50 g/2 oz/4 tbsp caster sugar, plus
   extra to decorate
175 g/6 oz/1½ cups plain flour
pinch of salt
24 whole blanched almonds, to
   decorate (optional)

butter

flour

caster sugar

almonds

1 Preheat the oven to 170°C/325°F/Gas 3. In a large bowl, beat together the butter and sugar until smooth. Mix in the flour and salt until the mixture resembles fine breadcrumbs.

2 With your hands, gather the mixture together to form a smooth dough (handle it as little as possible or the butter begins to become oily).

3 Press the dough evenly into a 20 cm/8 in loose-based flan tin (use your knuckles to press it firmly into the edges). Level the top with the back of a spoon.

4 Decorate the edge with the prongs of a fork and prick it all over. Cut the dough into wedges. Press in the almonds in a pattern, if you like. Bake for 40–50 minutes, or until the shortbread is a pale golden brown. Dust it with caster sugar while still warm. Let it cool in the tin for a few minutes, and then transfer it to a wire rack to cool completely.

Ginger Florentines

These colourful, chewy biscuits are delicious served with ice cream and are certain to disappear as soon as they are served. Store them in an airtight container.

Makes 30

INGREDIENTS
50 g/2 oz/4 tbsp butter
115 g/4 oz/8 tbsp caster sugar
50 g/2 oz/¼ cup mixed glacé cherries, chopped
25 g/1 oz/2 rounded tbsp candied orange peel, chopped
50 g/2 oz/½ cup flaked almonds
50 g/2 oz/½ cup chopped walnuts
25 g/1 oz/1 tbsp glacé ginger, chopped
30 ml/2 tbsp plain flour
2.5 ml/½ tsp ground ginger

TO FINISH
50 g/2 oz dark chocolate, or chocolate drops, melted
50 g/2 oz white chocolate, or chocolate drops, melted

walnuts

chocolate   caster sugar

orange peel   glacé cherries

glacé ginger

almonds

1 Preheat the oven to 180°C/350°F/ Gas 4. Whisk the butter and sugar together until they are light and fluffy. Thoroughly mix in all the remaining ingredients, except the melted chocolate.

2 Cut a piece of non-stick baking parchment to fit your baking trays. Put 4 small spoonfuls of the mixture on to each tray, spacing them well apart to allow for spreading. Flatten the biscuits and bake them for 5 minutes.

3 Remove the biscuits from the oven and flatten them with a wet fork, shaping them into neat rounds. Return to the oven for 3–4 minutes, until they are golden brown.

4 Let them cool on the baking trays for 2 minutes, to firm up, and then carefully transfer them to a wire rack. When they are cold and firm, spread the melted dark chocolate on the undersides of half the biscuits and spread the melted white chocolate on the undersides of the rest.

Chocolate Kisses

These rich little biscuits look attractive mixed together on a plate and dusted with icing sugar. Serve them with ice cream or simply with coffee.

Makes 24

INGREDIENTS
75 g/3 oz dark chocolate, broken into
   squares
75 g/3 oz white chocolate, broken
   into squares
115 g/4 oz/½ cup butter
115 g/4 oz/8 tbsp caster sugar
2 eggs
225 g/8 oz/2 cups plain flour
icing sugar, to decorate

icing sugar

flour

butter

eggs

chocolate

1 Put each chocolate into a small bowl and melt it over a pan of hot, but not boiling, water. Set aside to cool.

2 Whisk together the butter and caster sugar until they are pale and fluffy. Beat in the eggs, one at a time. Then sift in the flour and mix well.

3 Halve the mixture and divide it between the two bowls of chocolate. Mix each chocolate in thoroughly. Knead the doughs until smooth, wrap them in clear film and chill them for 1 hour. Preheat the oven to 190°C/375°F/Gas 5.

4 Shape slightly rounded teaspoonfuls of both doughs roughly into balls. Roll the balls in the palms of your hands to make neater ball shapes. Arrange the balls on greased baking trays and bake them for 10–12 minutes. Dust with sifted icing sugar and then transfer them to a wire rack to cool.

Filo Crackers

These can be prepared a day in advance, brushed with melted butter and kept covered with clear film in the fridge or freezer before baking.

Makes about 24

INGREDIENTS
2 × 275 g/10 oz packet frozen filo
  pastry, thawed
115 g/4 oz/½ cup butter, melted
thin foil ribbon, to decorate
sifted icing sugar, to decorate

FOR THE FILLING
450 g/1 lb dessert apples, peeled,
  cored and finely chopped
5 ml/1 tsp ground cinnamon
25 g/1 oz/2 tbsp soft light brown sugar
50 g/2 oz/½ cup pecan nuts, chopped
50 g/2 oz/1 cup fresh white
  breadcrumbs
25 g/1 oz/3 tbsp sultanas
25 g/1 oz/3 heaped tbsp currants

FOR THE LEMON SAUCE
115 g/4 oz caster sugar
finely grated rind of 1 lemon
juice of 2 lemons

filo pastry

brown sugar

caster sugar

lemons

1 Unwrap the filo pastry and cover it with clear film and a damp cloth, to prevent it from drying out. Put the chopped apples in a bowl and mix in the remaining filling ingredients.

2 Take one sheet of pastry at a time and cut it into 15 × 30 cm/6 × 12 in strips. Brush with butter. Place a spoonful of the filling at one end and fold in the sides, so the pastry measures 13 cm/5 in across. Brush the edges with butter and roll up. Pinch the 'frill' at either end and tie with ribbon. Brush with butter.

3 Place the crackers on baking trays, cover and chill for 10 minutes. Preheat the oven to 190°C/375°F/Gas 5. Brush each cracker with melted butter. Bake the crackers for 30–35 minutes, or until they are golden brown. Let them cool slightly on the baking trays and then transfer them to a wire rack to cool completely.

4 To make the lemon sauce, put all the ingredients in a small pan and heat gently to dissolve the sugar. Serve the sauce warm, in a sauce boat. Finally, dust the crackers with sifted icing sugar and arrange them on a serving plate.

INDEX